Dollar Bill Origami

Other books by John Montroll:

Origami Sculptures

Prehistoric Origami *Dinosaurs and Other Creatures*

Origami Sea Life by John Montroll and Robert J. Lang

African Animals in Origami

North American Animals in Origami

Mythological Creatures and the Chinese Zodiac in Origami

Teach Yourself Origami

Bringing Origami to Life

Dollar Bill Animals in Origami

Bugs and Birds in Origami

A Plethora of Polyhedra in Origami

A Constellation of Origami Polyhedra

Christmas Origami

Animal Origami for the Enthusiast

Origami for the Enthusiast

Easy Origami

Birds in Origami

Favorite Animals in Origami

Easy Christmas Origami

Dollar Bill Origami

John Montroll

Dover Publications, Inc.
New York

To Al, Lauren, Andrew, and Robert

Copyright

Copyright © 2003 by John Montroll
All rights reserved.

Bibliographical Note

This work is first published in 2003 in separate editions by
Antroll Publishing Company, Maryland, and Dover Publications,
Inc., New York.

Library of Congress Cataloging-in-Publication Data

Montroll, John.
    Dollar bill origami : John Montroll.
        p. cm.
    ISBN 0-486-42982-2 (pbk.)
    1. Origami. 2. Dollar, American.   I. Title.
TT870.M5535 2003
736'.982—dc22

                                                                    2003055485

        Manufactured in the United States of America
Dover Publications, Inc., 31 East 2nd Street, Mineola, N.Y. 11501

INTRODUCTION

For years, origami enthusiasts have used the dollar bill as the basis for many creations. From animals to flowers, bugs to trees, the dollar bill has steadily gained popularity as a unique type of origami paper. Proportionally well suited to paperfolding, there seems to be no end to the many different types of models one can fold.

Since the publication of my book, *Dollar Bill Animals in Origami*, many folders have expressed an interest in this genre. I am pleased to present this sequel, which features the creations of a number of my colleagues as well as my own designs.

There is something for every level of paperfolding in this collection, from the simple boat by Sy Chen to the complex dragonfly by Won Park. Along the way you can fold a windmill (by Sy Chen), shirt with tie (by Stefan Delecat), tulip (by Mark Kennedy), eagle (by Wong Park), and armadillo (by Jim Cowling). There is even an African mask (by Matt Slayton) and some polyhedra. For those models designed by others, the name of the designer is listed at the beginning of the instructions; uncredited designs are my own.

It is up to you which side of the dollar bill should show in finished models. Although the diagrams use white and shading to represent the dollar bill's two sides, you may choose which side of the bill you wish to show; generally, the diagrams will show predominantly the shaded side. However, the final drawings of each model are completely shaded and do not distinguish between the two sides.

Of course you do not need to fold from dollar bills. Any paper can easily be cut to form the proportions of a bill. One method, shown on page 10, shows an easy way to approximate the proportions given a square or rectangle. The illustrations conform to the internationally accepted Randlett-Yoshizawa conventions. Origami paper can be found in many hobby shops or purchased by mail from OrigamiUSA, 15 West 77th Street, New York, NY 10024-5192 or from Dover Publications, Inc., 31 East 2nd Street, Mineola, NY 11501. Large sheets are easier to use than small ones.

I wish to thank the origami community for encouraging me to write this book. Special thanks go to the contributors—Sy Chen, Jim Cowling, Stefan Delecat, Peter Farina, Gay Merrill Gross, Stephen Hecht, Mark Kennedy, Robert J. Lang, Won Park, Matt Slayton, and Mike Thomas. Thanks to my editor Charley Montroll. Of course I also thank the many folders who proofread the diagrams.

John Montroll

CONTENTS

★ Simple
★★ Intermediate
★★★ Complex

Boat
★
page 11

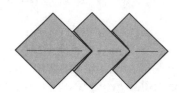

Three Diamonds
★
page 13

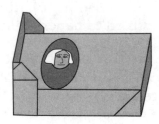

George Washington Slept Here
★
page 15

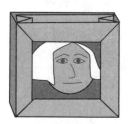

George Washington Framed
★★
page 17

Star of David
★★
page 19

Windmill
★★
page 21

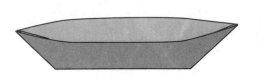

House with Chimney
★★
page 24

Sword
★★
page 27

"One-Way" Arrow
★★
page 30

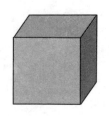

Tetrahedron
★★
page 34

Cube
★★
page 36

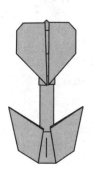

Diamond
★★
page 39

Tulip
★★
page 42

Evergreen
★★
page 49

Tree
★★
page 46

Flower
★★★
page 48

African Mask
★★
page 53

Shirt with Tie
★★
page 56

Swan
★
page 60

Crane
★★
page 62

Vulture
★★
page 64

Goose
★★
page 67

Flamingo
★★
page 70

Peacock
★★
page 73

Pelican
★★
page 76

More →

Dollar Bill Origami 7

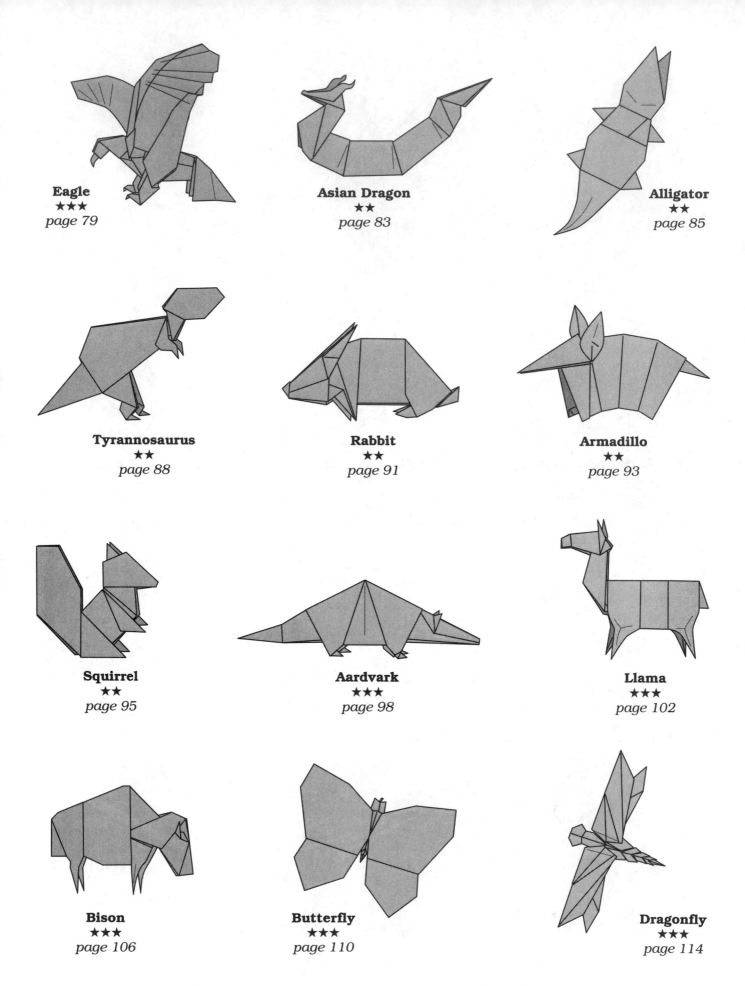

Eagle
★★★
page 79

Asian Dragon
★★
page 83

Alligator
★★
page 85

Tyrannosaurus
★★
page 88

Rabbit
★★
page 91

Armadillo
★★
page 93

Squirrel
★★
page 95

Aardvark
★★★
page 98

Llama
★★★
page 102

Bison
★★★
page 106

Butterfly
★★★
page 110

Dragonfly
★★★
page 114

SYMBOLS

Lines

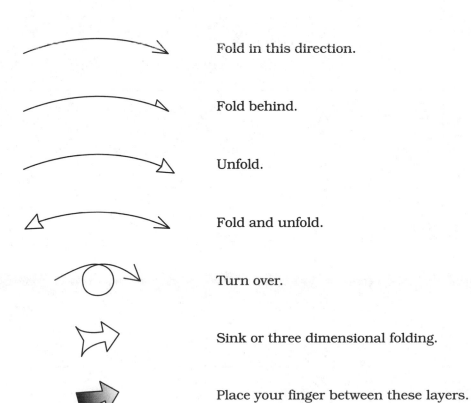

– – – – – – – – – –	Valley fold, fold in front.
– ·· – · – · – · – · –	Mountain fold, fold behind.
————————	Crease line.
	X-ray or guide line.

Arrows

	Fold in this direction.
	Fold behind.
	Unfold.
	Fold and unfold.
	Turn over.
	Sink or three dimensional folding.
	Place your finger between these layers.

DOLLAR BILLS FROM A SQUARE

The dollar bill has dimensions of approximately 2.59 inches by 6.094 inches. This ratio is 1 by 2.35. There are two simple, approximate methods of cutting any square or rectangle to have the proportions of a dollar bill. One is to use the dimensions 3 by 7 (1 by 2.333). Another method is to create a rectangle with the diagonal at a 22.5° angle as shown here; the ratio for this method is approximately 1 by 2.414.

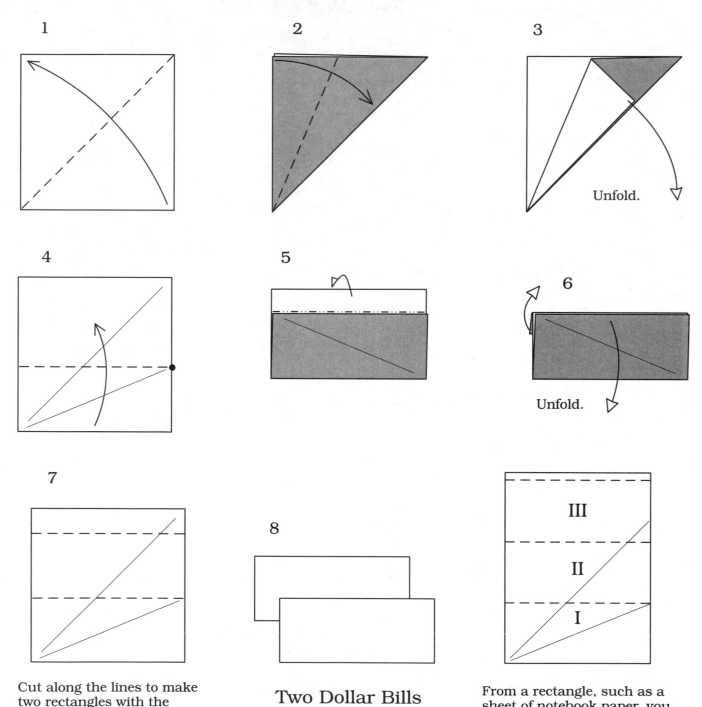

Cut along the lines to make two rectangles with the proportions of a dollar bill.

Two Dollar Bills

From a rectangle, such as a sheet of notebook paper, you can make three rectangles with the proportions of a dollar bill.

BOAT

Designed by Sy Chen

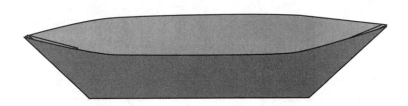

1

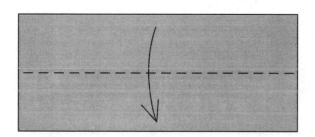

2

Repeat behind.

3

Fold and unfold. Do not repeat behind.

4

Reverse-fold.

5

Tuck inside.

6

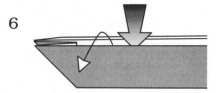

Open to view
the inside.

7

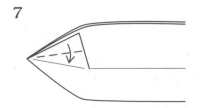

This is a view
of the inside.

8

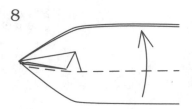

9

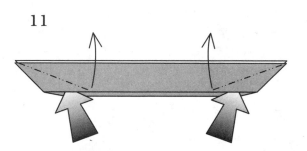

10

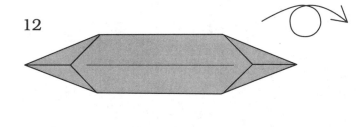

Repeat steps 3–8.

11

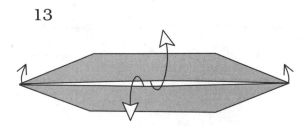

Open with squash
folds on each side.

12

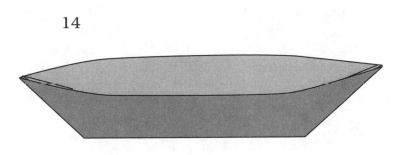

13

Open the boat.

14

Boat

THREE DIAMONDS

Designed by Mike Thomas

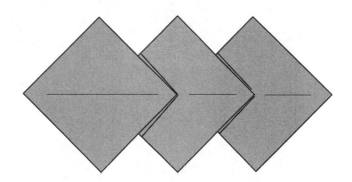

1

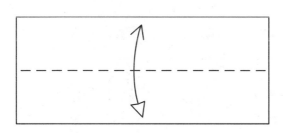

Fold and unfold. Rotate.

2

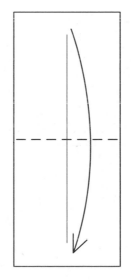

3

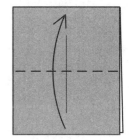

Repeat behind.

4

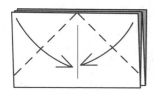

Repeat behind.

5

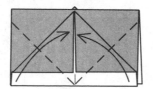

Repeat behind.

6

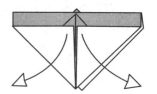

Unfold. Repeat behind.

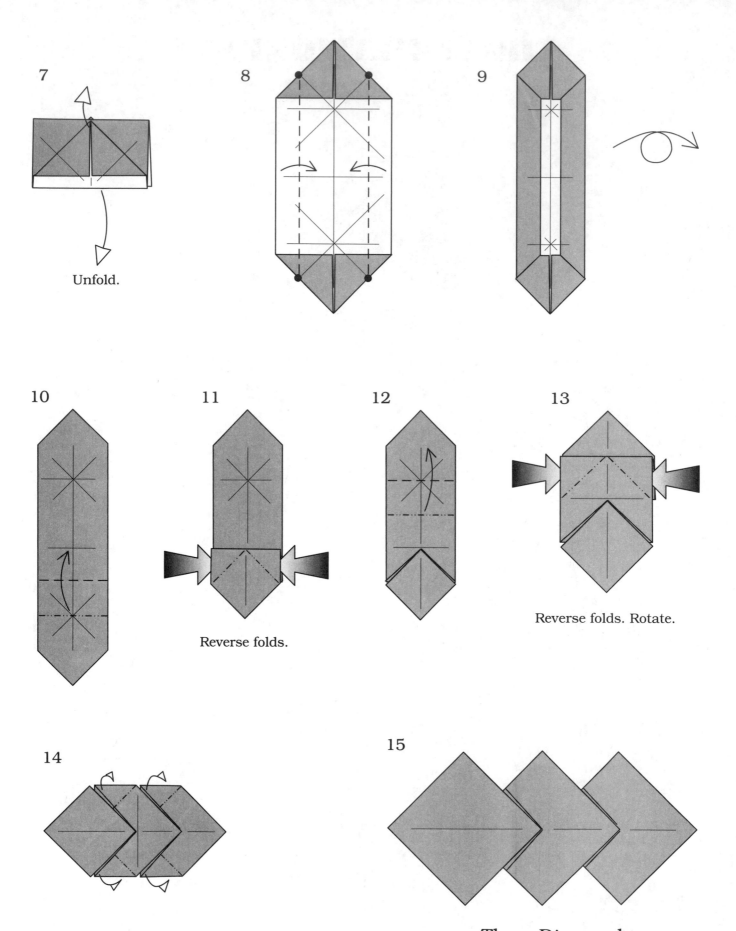

7

Unfold.

8

9

10

11

Reverse folds.

12

13

Reverse folds. Rotate.

14

15

Three Diamonds

GEORGE WASHINGTON SLEPT HERE

Designed by Gay Merrill Gross

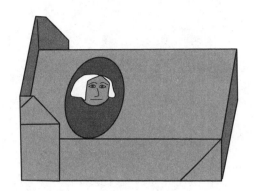

Begin with the
"ONE" on the front.

1

Fold and unfold,
creasing at the ends.

2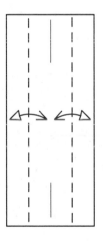

Fold and unfold.

3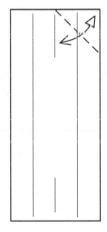

Fold and unfold,
creasing lightly.

4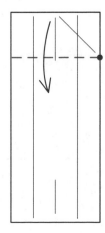

5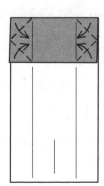

6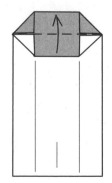

7

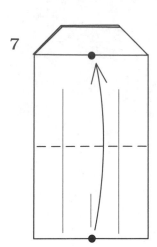

8

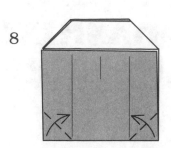

9

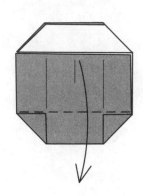

10

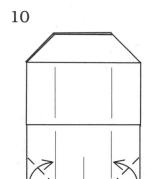

11

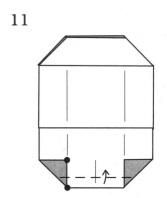

Fold up about one-third of
the way between the dots.

12

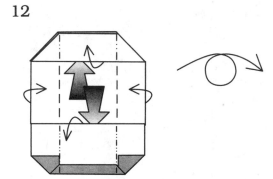

Open to form the bed.

13

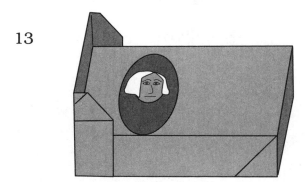

George Washington Slept Here

GEORGE WASHINGTON FRAMED

Designed by Gay Merrill Gross

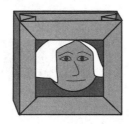

Begin with George Washington
on the front.

1
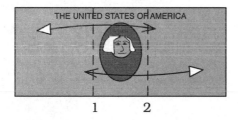

Line 1 runs through the end of the first
bar in the letter "E" in UNITED. Fold
and unfold. Line 2 runs through the
very end of "F" in OF. Fold and unfold.

2

Fold and unfold,
creasing at the ends.

3
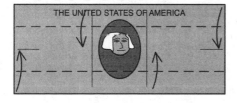

4
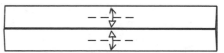

Fold and unfold the edges from
the center to the top or bottom.
Only crease at the center around
Washington's face.

5
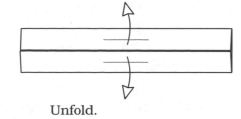

Unfold.

6
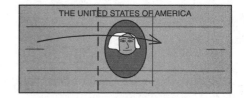

Fold along the existing crease.

7

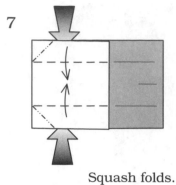

Squash folds.

8

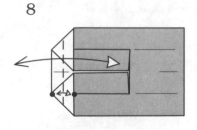

Fold to the left and
unfold. Do not crease
the bottom layer.

9

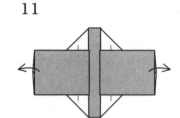

10

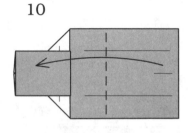

Repeat steps 6–9 on
the other side.

11

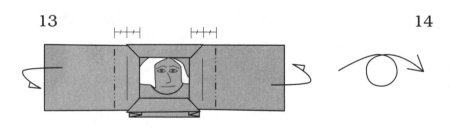

Pull the opposite flaps
to open into a box.

12

Collapse the box by refolding
along existing creases.

13

Note the width of the frame side.

14

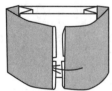

Tuck inside.

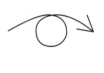

15

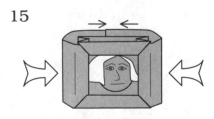

Push in both sides at the same time. With
one finger, press Washington's portrait so
that it touches the back of the frame.

16

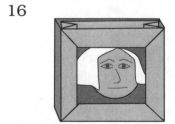

George Washington Framed

STAR OF DAVID

Designed by Sy Chen

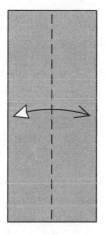

1

Fold and unfold.

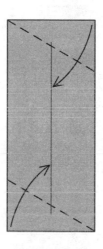

2

Fold to the center line.

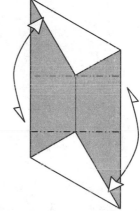

3

Fold and unfold.

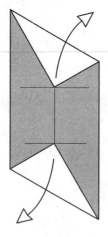

4

Unfold.

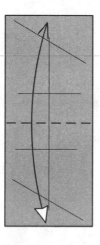

5

Fold in half and unfold.

6

7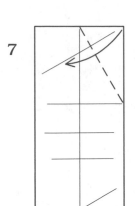

8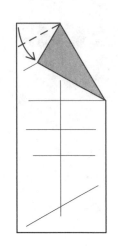

9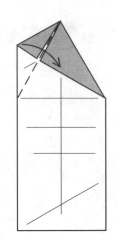

10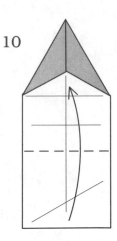

11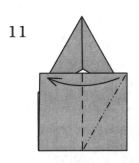

Squash-fold.

12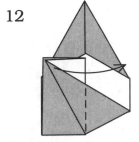

13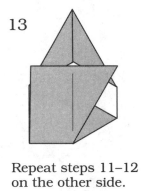

Repeat steps 11–12 on the other side.

14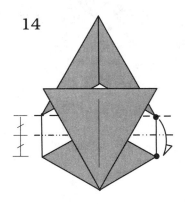

15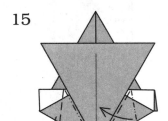

Squash folds.

16

Bring the dark paper to the front.

17

Place the white paper on the right under the darker layer.

18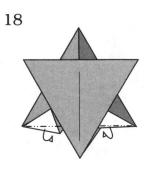

Tuck inside.

19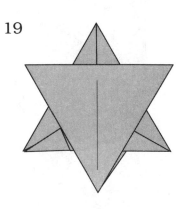

Star of David

WINDMILL

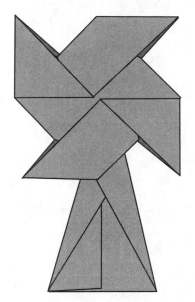

Designed by Sy Chen

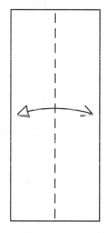

1

Fold and unfold.

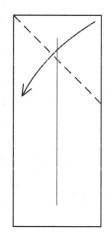

2

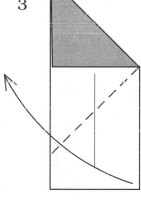

3

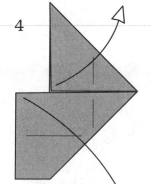

4

Unfold.

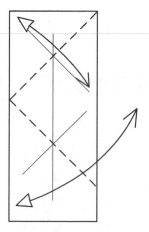

5

Fold and unfold.

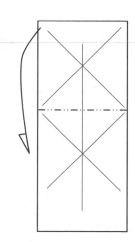

6

7

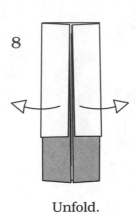

8

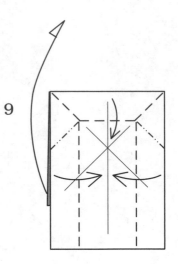

Unfold.

9

Lift up from behind
while closing in front.

10

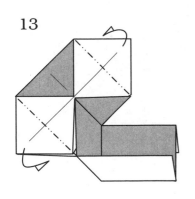

11

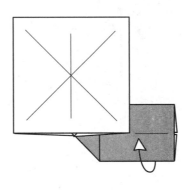

Wrap the paper around.

12

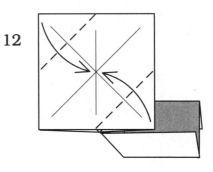

13

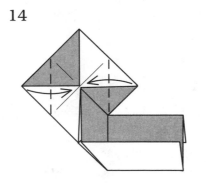

14

15

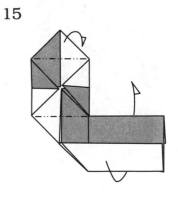

16

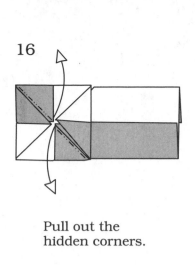

Pull out the
hidden corners.

17

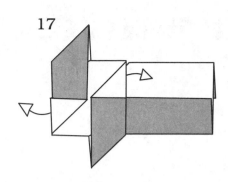

Pull out from behind.

18

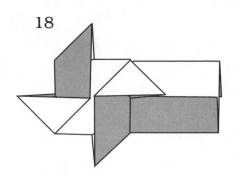

Turn over and rotate.

19

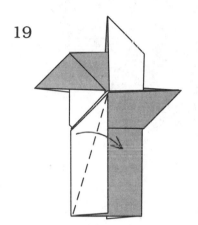

20

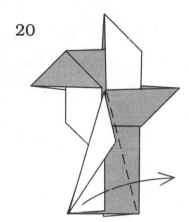

21

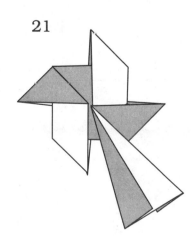

Turn over and rotate.

22

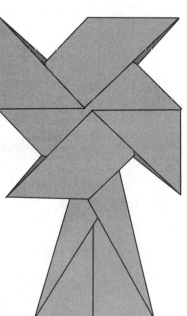

Windmill

HOUSE WITH CHIMNEY

Designed by Sy Chen

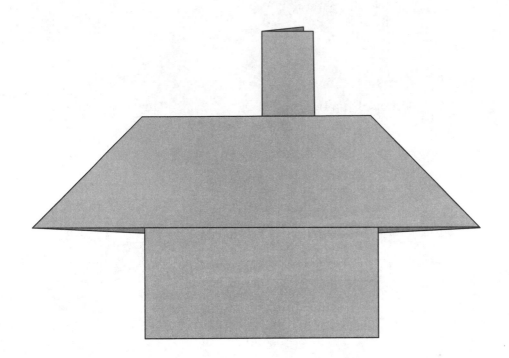

1

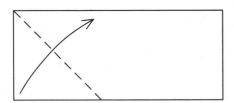

2

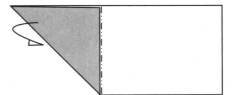

3

4

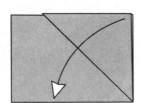

5

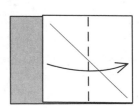

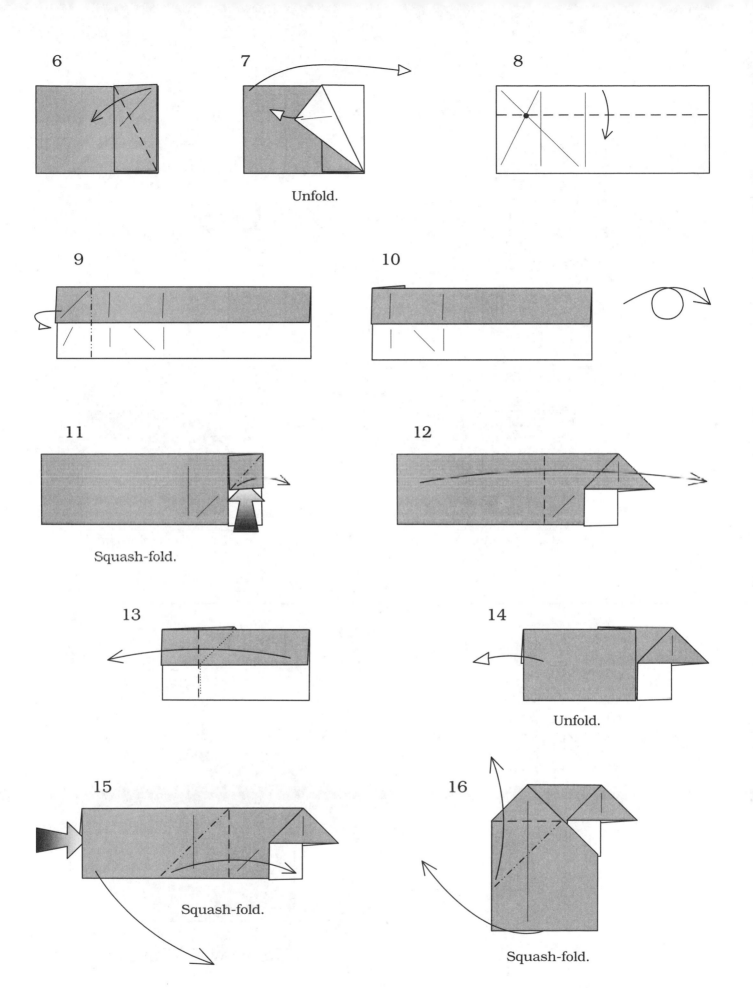

6

7

Unfold.

8

9

10

11

Squash-fold.

12

13

14

Unfold.

15

Squash-fold.

16

Squash-fold.

17

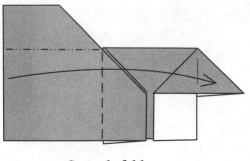

Squash-fold.

18

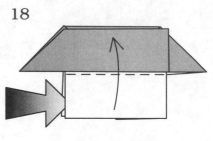

Squash-fold.

19

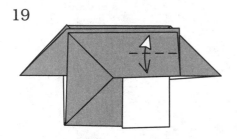

Fold and unfold.

20

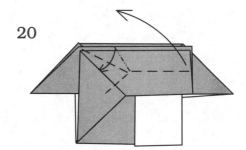

Rabbit-ear.

21

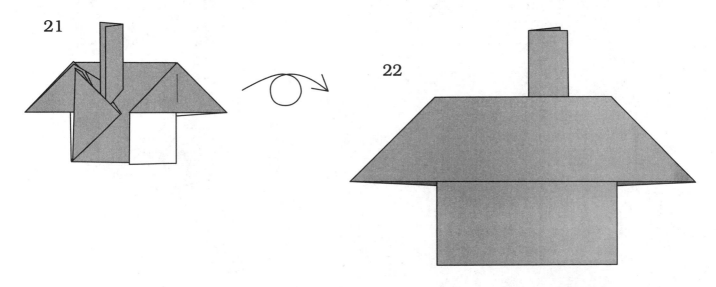

22

House with Chimney

SWORD

Designed by Peter Farina

1

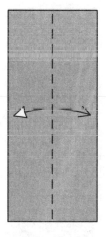

Fold and unfold.

2

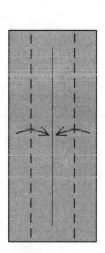

3

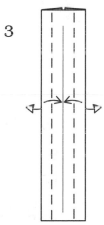

4

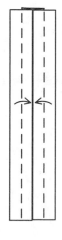

5

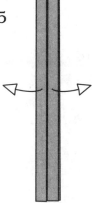

Unfold.

6

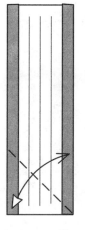

Fold and unfold.

7

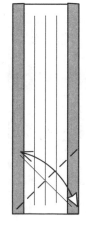

Fold and unfold.

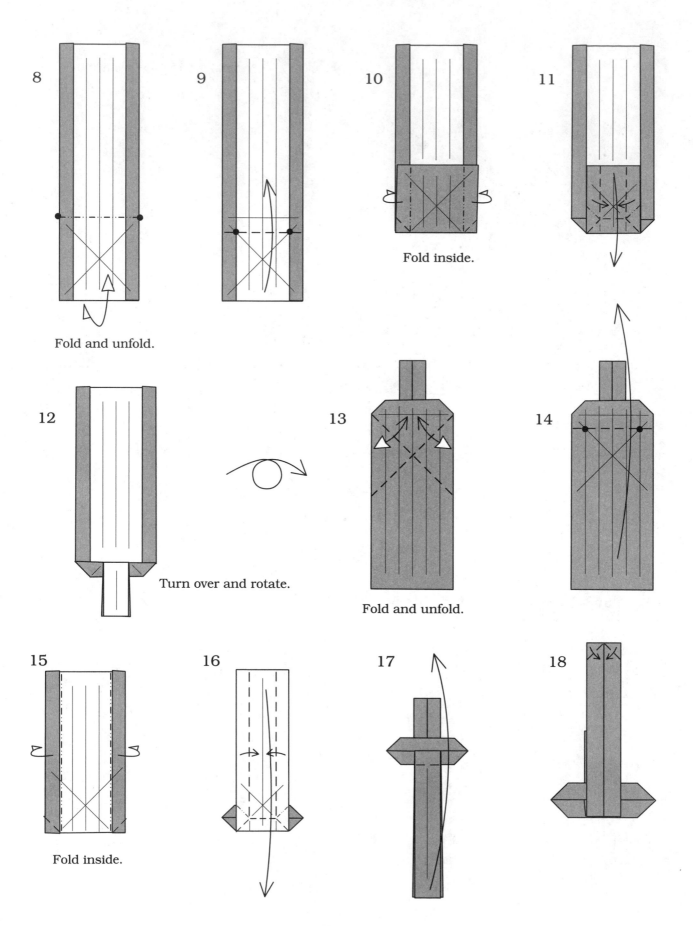

8

Fold and unfold.

9

10

Fold inside.

11

12

Turn over and rotate.

13

Fold and unfold.

14

15

Fold inside.

16

17

18

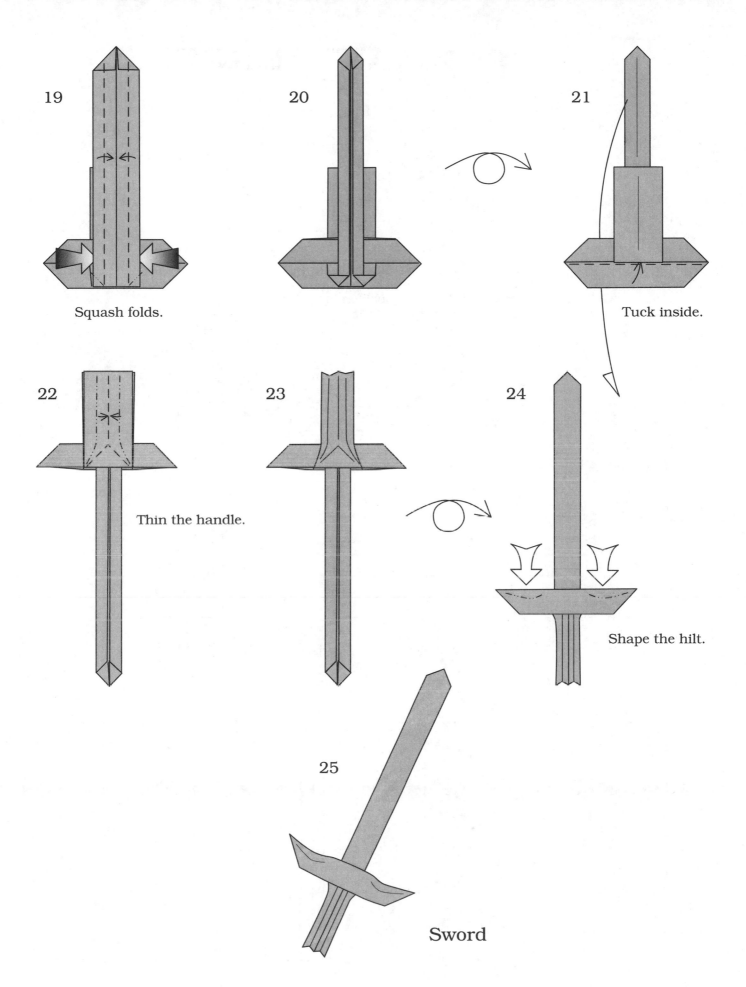

19 Squash folds.

20

21 Tuck inside.

22 Thin the handle.

23

24 Shape the hilt.

25

Sword

"ONE-WAY" ARROW

Designed by Stephen Hecht

This arrow can also be folded from rectangles of other dimensions, provided they are considerably longer than they are wide.

1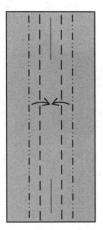

Begin with the "ONE" on the front.

2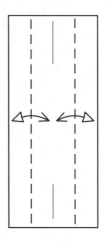

Fold and unfold, creasing at the ends.

3

Fold and unfold.

4

5

6

Unfold.

7

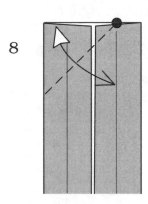

8

The top will form the "point" of the arrow. Fold and unfold all the layers.

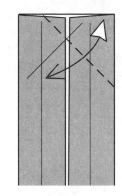

9

Fold and unfold.

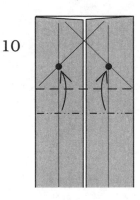

10

Pleat. Make the valley fold first. Then bring the mountain fold to the indicated intersections.

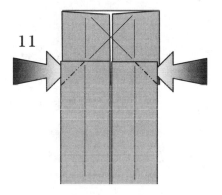

11

Reverse folds.

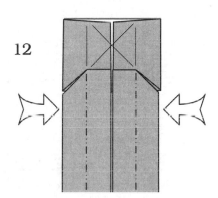

12

Reverse-fold the long edges, closed-sinking at the top corners.

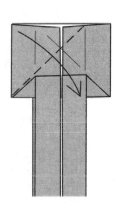

13

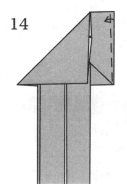

14

Fold a very thin layer.

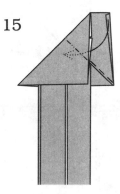

15

Reverse-fold the other corner on existing creases, tucking into the triangle on the left. The thin fold at the right edge helps make the tuck easier.

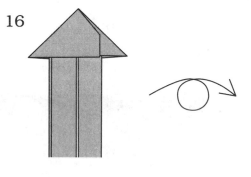

16

The "point" of the arrow is finished. Turn over and rotate.

17

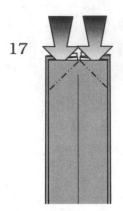

Begin working on the "flights". Reverse-fold the top layers.

18

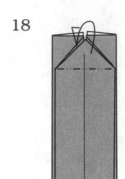

Spread slightly to sink inside.

19

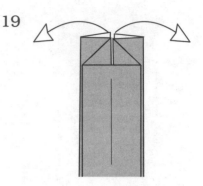

Unfold the edges from behind. The model is not flat at the "point" end.

20

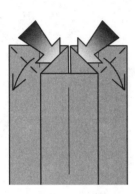

Reverse folds.

21

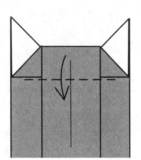

22

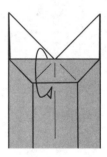

Open the model a bit to wrap around.

23

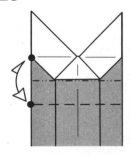

First mountain fold along the bottom of the trapezoid, then valley fold. Unfold.

24

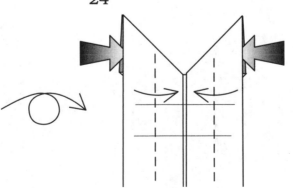

Fold to the center keeping the top three-dimensional.

25

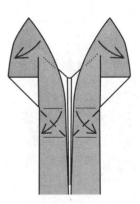

Valley-fold the top layer, between pleat lines, which lifts the "flights" perpendicular.

26

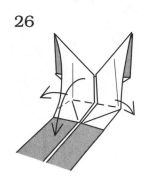

Continue flipping over
the "flights" in this
three-dimensional step.

27

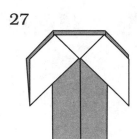

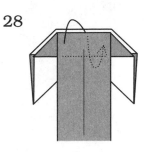

28

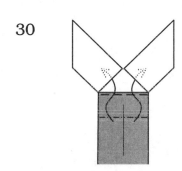

Tuck inside the
hidden trapezoid.

29

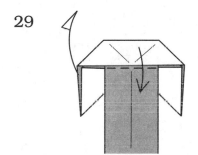

30

Pleat and tuck under the diagonal
edges. Gently bend the model along the
vertical with a mountain fold to facilitate
the tuck. Then flatten out to secure.

31

"One-Way" Arrow

TETRAHEDRON

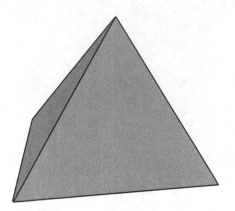

1

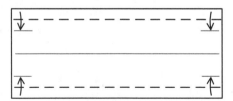

Fold and unfold.

2

Fold and unfold.

3

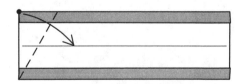

4

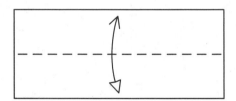

Fold the corner
to the crease.

5

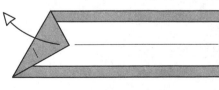

Unfold.

6

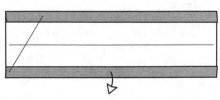

Unfold.

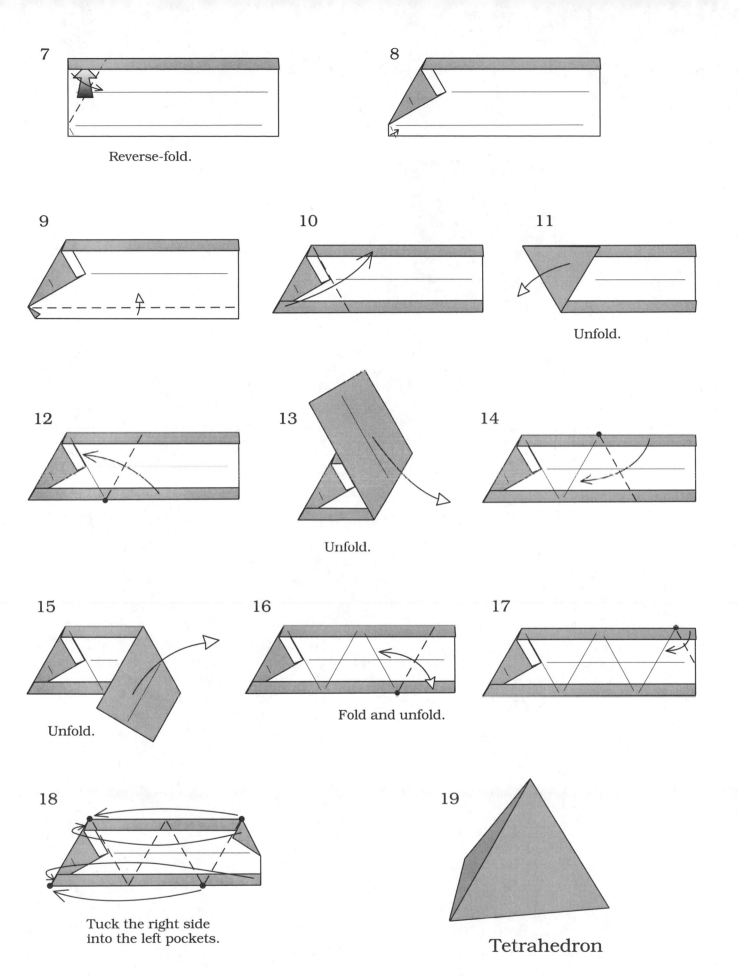

7

Reverse-fold.

8

9

10

11

Unfold.

12

13

Unfold.

14

15

Unfold.

16

Fold and unfold.

17

18

Tuck the right side
into the left pockets.

19

Tetrahedron

CUBE

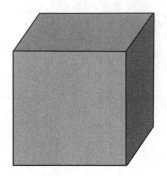

1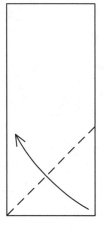

2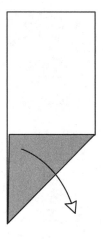

Unfold.

3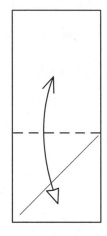

Fold and unfold.

4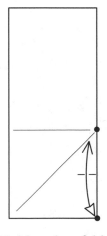

Fold and unfold.

5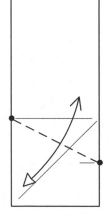

Fold and unfold.

6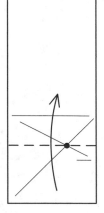

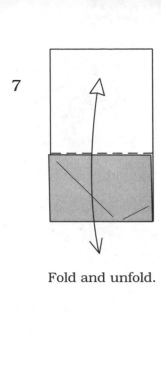

7

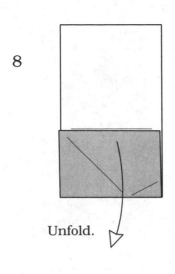

8

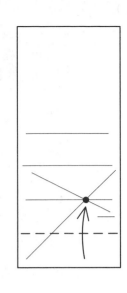

9

Fold and unfold.

Unfold.

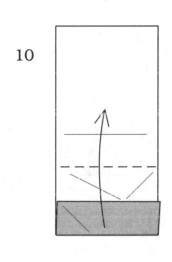

10

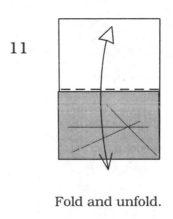

11

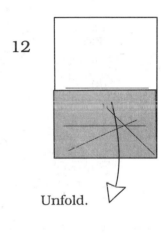

12

Fold and unfold.

Unfold.

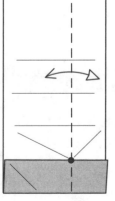

13

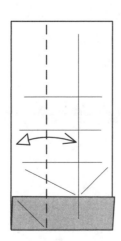

14

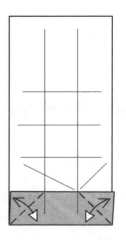

15

Fold and unfold.

Fold to the crease
and unfold.

Fold and unfold
both layers.

16

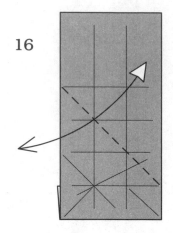

Fold and unfold.

17

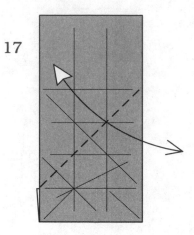

Fold and unfold.

18

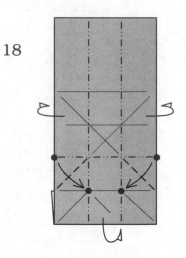

The model will become three-dimensional.

19

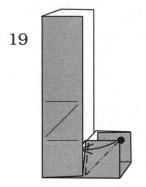

Tuck inside.
Repeat behind.

20

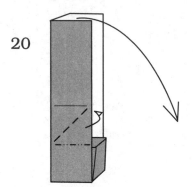

Repeat behind
to flatten the
paper at the top

21

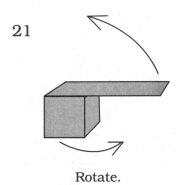

Rotate.

22

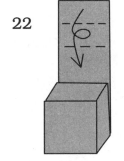

23

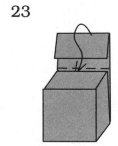

Tuck inside.

24

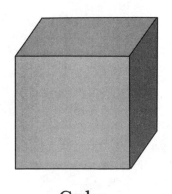

Cube

DIAMOND

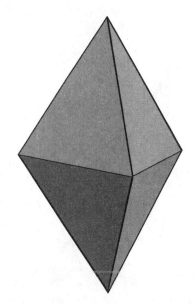

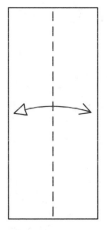

1

Fold and unfold.

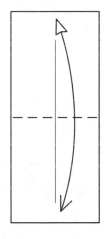

2

Fold and unfold.

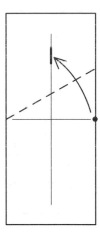

3

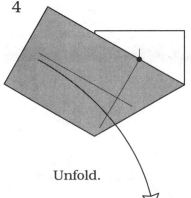

4

Unfold.

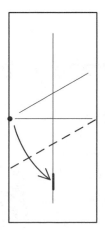

5

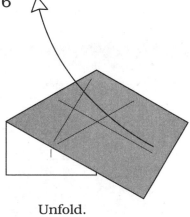

6

Unfold.

7

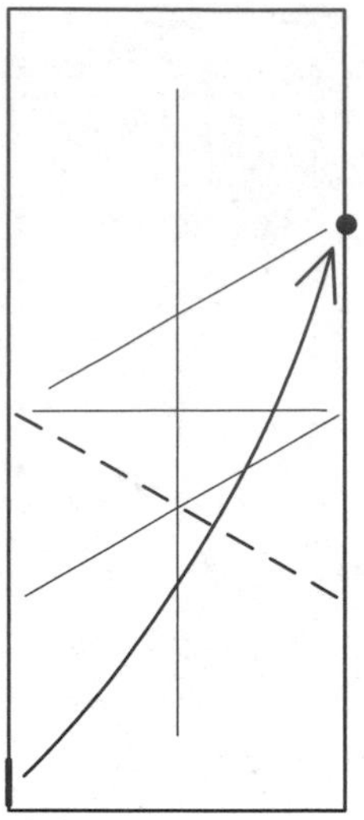

8

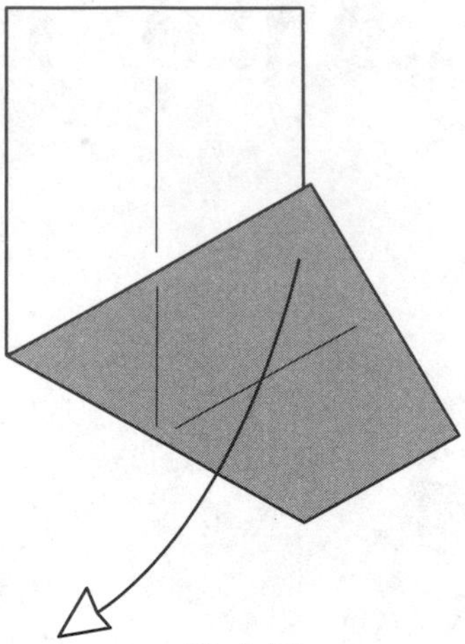

Unfold.

9

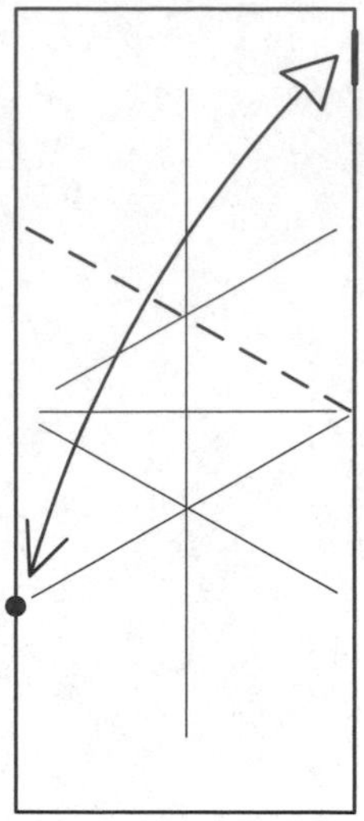

Fold and unfold.

10

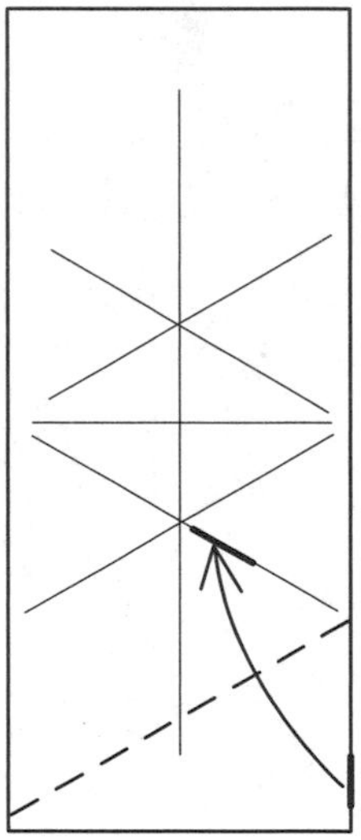

11

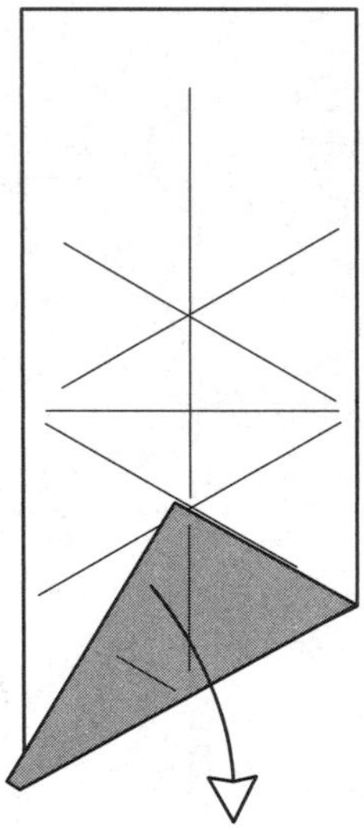

Unfold.

12

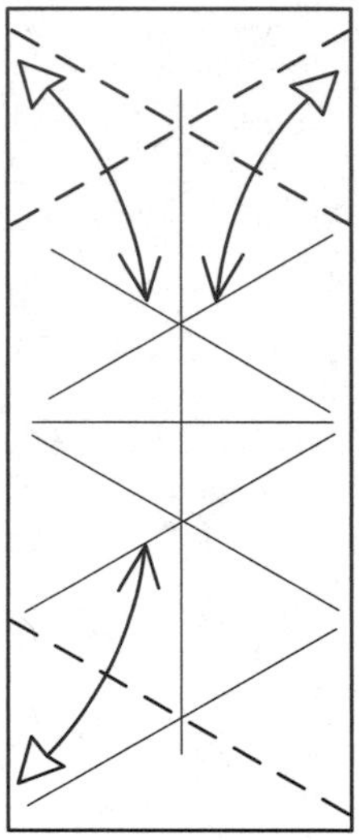

Fold and
unfold. Rotate.

13

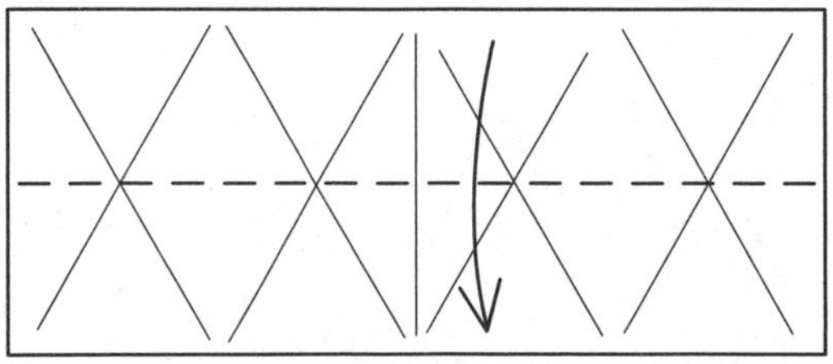

14

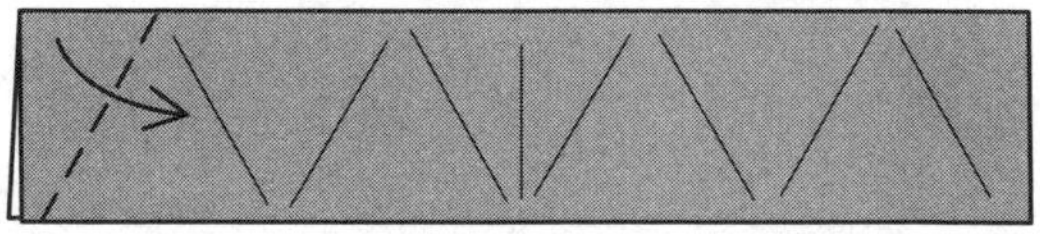

15

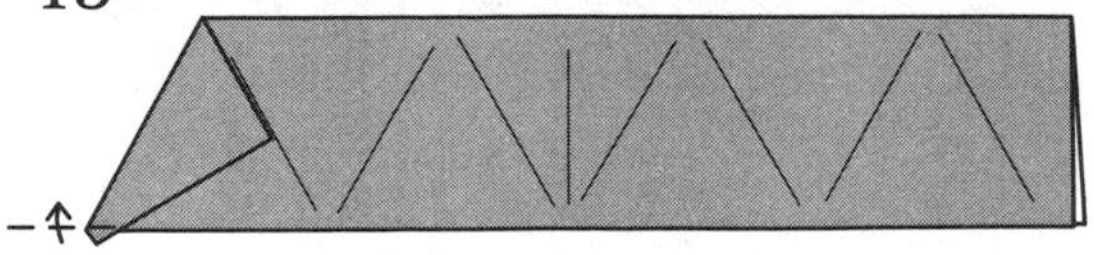

16

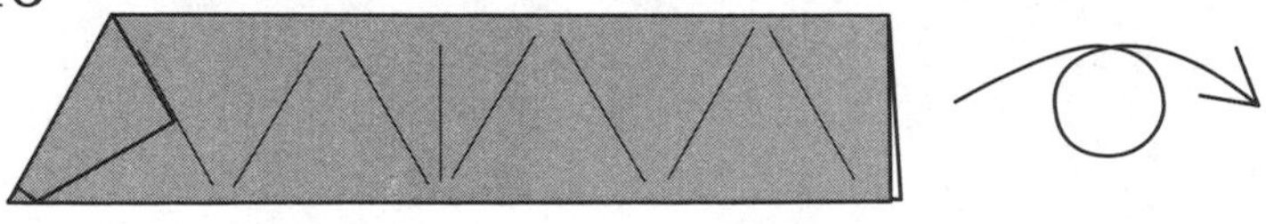

17

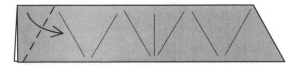

Repeat steps 14–15.

18

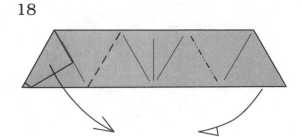

19

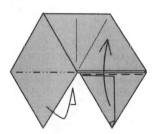

Fold behind on the left
and in front on the right.

20

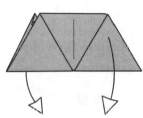

Unfold.

21

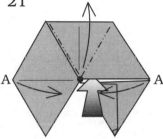

Bring the two A's together
while the center dot goes up.
The model will become
three-dimensional. Rotate.

22

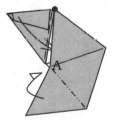

Tuck inside at the
top and bottom.

23

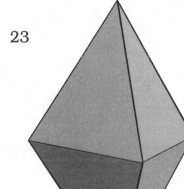

Diamond

TULIP

Designed by Mark Kennedy

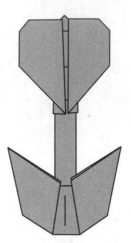

1

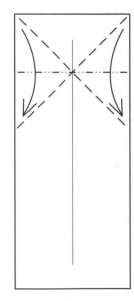

Fold and unfold.
Rotate.

2

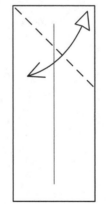

Fold and unfold.

3

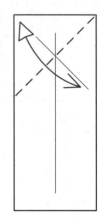

Fold and unfold.

4

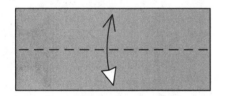

5

Repeat steps 2–4
on the bottom.

6

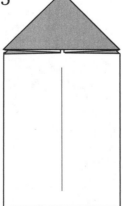

7

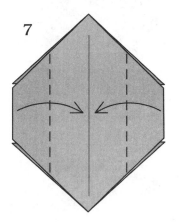

8

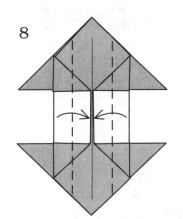

9

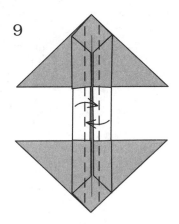

Fold in thirds.

10

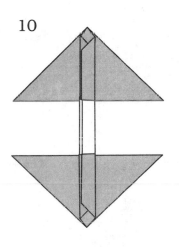

11

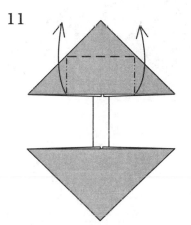

Petal-fold.

12

Petal-fold behind.

13

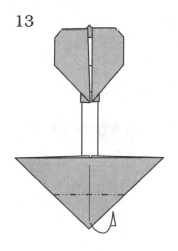

14

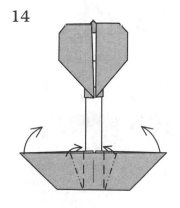

15

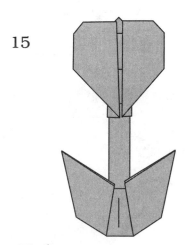

Tulip

Tulip 43

EVERGREEN

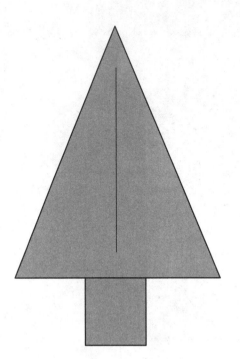

1

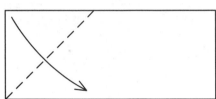

2

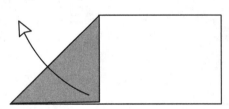

Unfold.

3

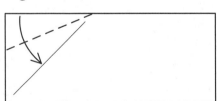

4

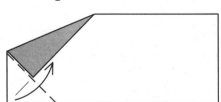

5

6

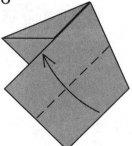

7

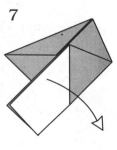

Unfold.

8

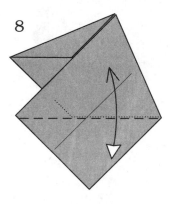

Fold and unfold.

9

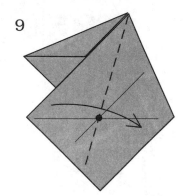

10

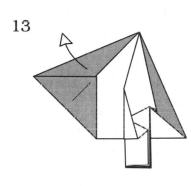

Squash-fold so
the dots meet.

11

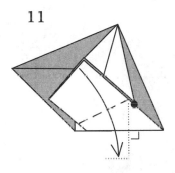

Fold slightly above the
dot. Note the right angle.

12

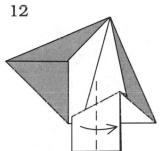

13

Unfold.

14

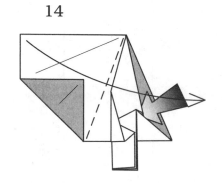

Note the pocket.

15

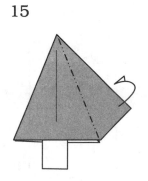

Tuck inside
the pocket.

16

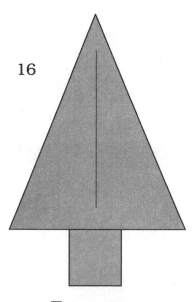

Evergreen

TREE

1  Fold and unfold.

2 Fold and unfold.

3 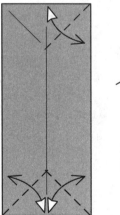 Fold and unfold.

4 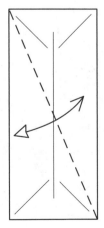 Fold and unfold.

5  Fold and unfold.

6 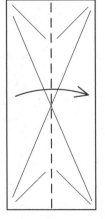 Fold in half and rotate.

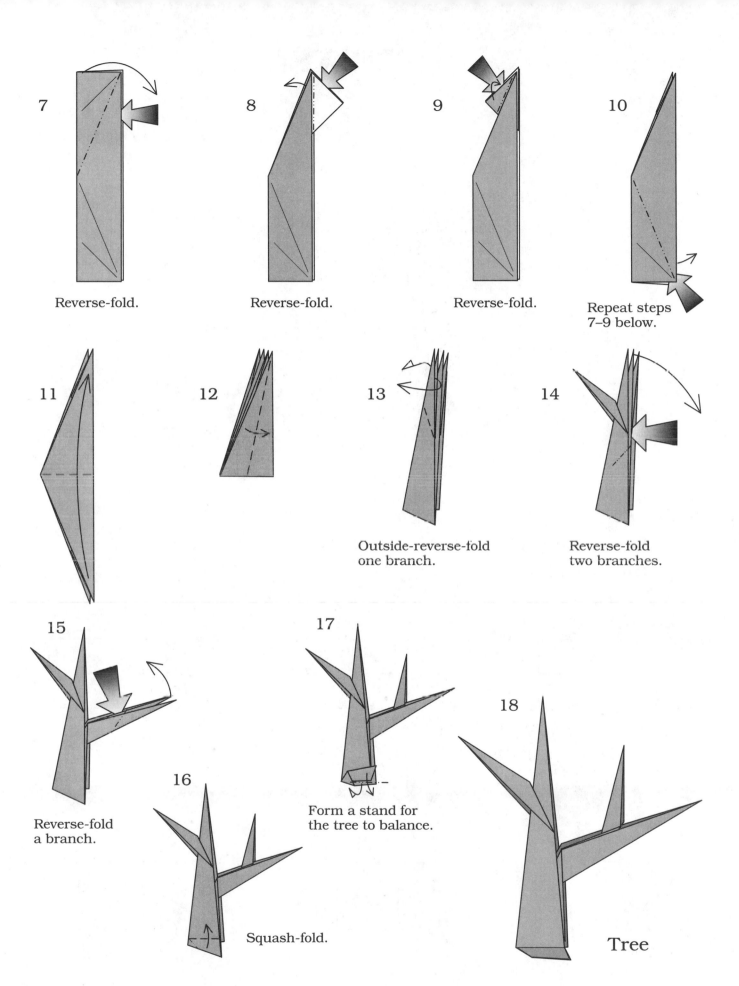

7

Reverse-fold.

8

Reverse-fold.

9

Reverse-fold.

10

Repeat steps
7–9 below.

11

12

13

Outside-reverse-fold
one branch.

14

Reverse-fold
two branches.

15

Reverse-fold
a branch.

16

Squash-fold.

17

Form a stand for
the tree to balance.

18

Tree

FLOWER

Designed by Stephen Hecht

1

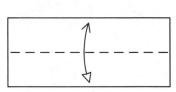

Fold and unfold.

2

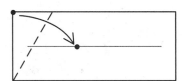

3

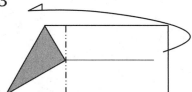

4

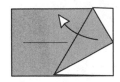

Unfold.

5

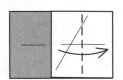

6

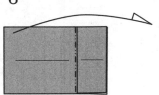

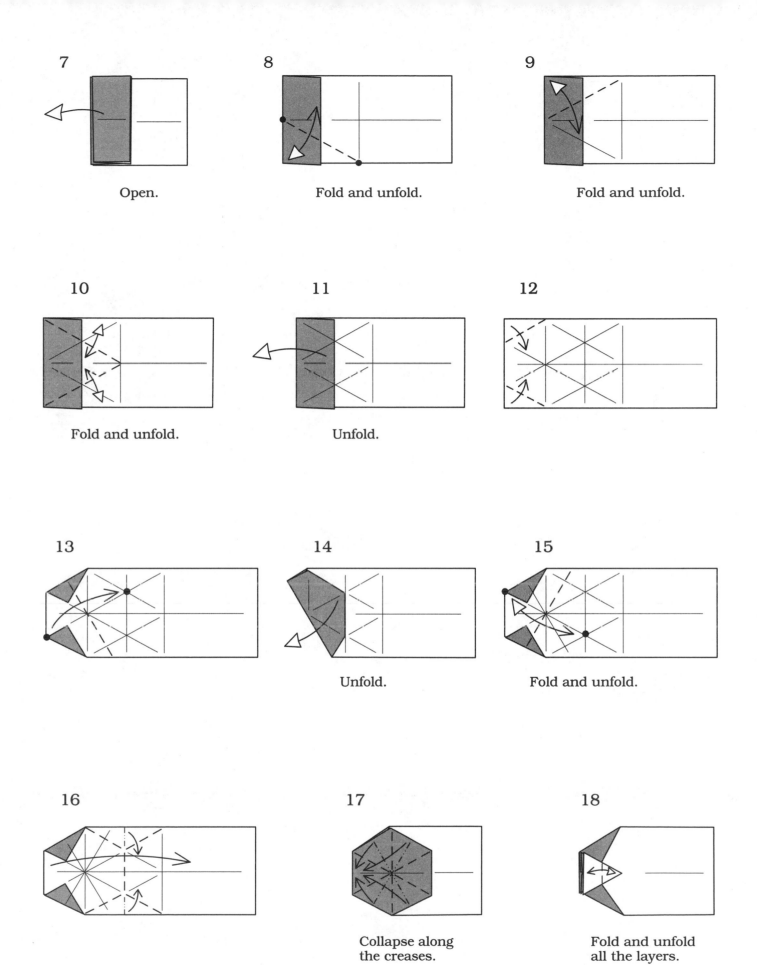

7

Open.

8

Fold and unfold.

9

Fold and unfold.

10

Fold and unfold.

11

Unfold.

12

13

14

Unfold.

15

Fold and unfold.

16

17

Collapse along
the creases.

18

Fold and unfold
all the layers.

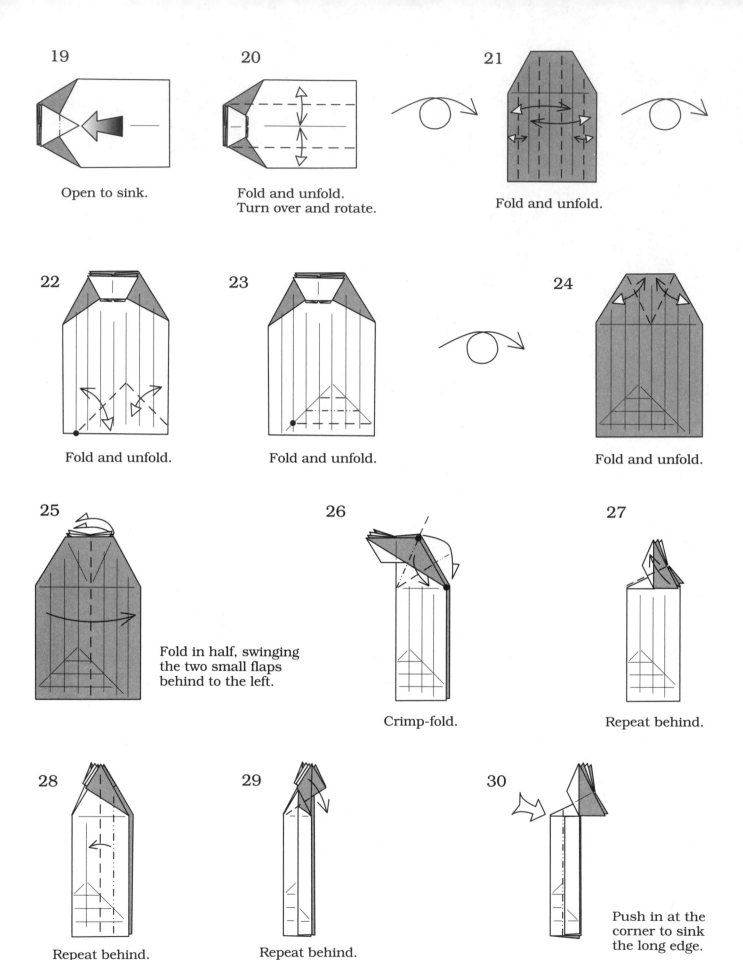

19

Open to sink.

20

Fold and unfold.
Turn over and rotate.

21

Fold and unfold.

22

Fold and unfold.

23

Fold and unfold.

24

Fold and unfold.

25

Fold in half, swinging
the two small flaps
behind to the left.

26

Crimp-fold.

27

Repeat behind.

28

Repeat behind.

29

Repeat behind.

30

Push in at the
corner to sink
the long edge.

31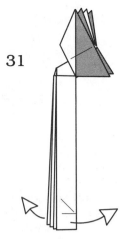

Spread at the bottom
and view the left side
in the next step.

32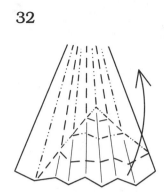

Spread pleats,
refold along the
existing creases.

33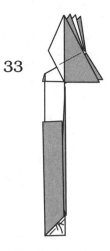

Tuck inside.

34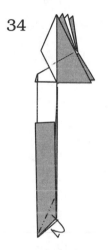

Tuck inside.
Repeat behind.

35

36

Tuck inside.

37

38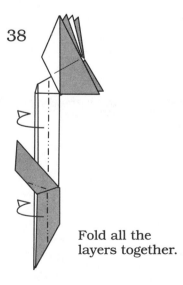

Fold all the
layers together.

39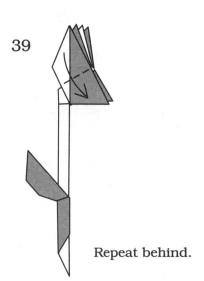

Repeat behind.

40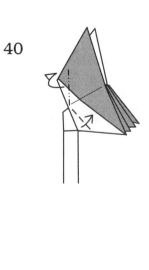

Flower 51

41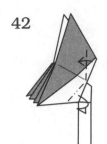

42

43

Reverse-fold the top edges of all six petals (about one-third of the angle). Do not flatten.

44

This is a veiw from above the bloom. Pull down the tips of the petals while gently flattening the cente.

45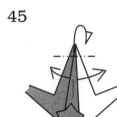

This is a single petal. Open and round the sides of the petal, and mountain-fold the tip behind. Flatten the underside of the petal, especially the thick petals adjoining the stem.

46

Flower

AFRICAN MASK

Designed by Matt Slayton

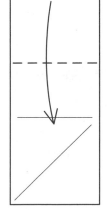

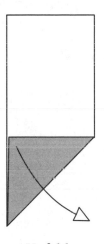

1

2

Unfold.

3

Fold and unfold.

4

Fold down slightly
below the line.

5

Unfold.

6

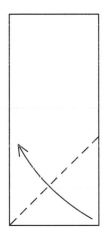

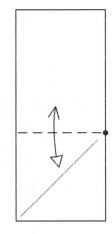

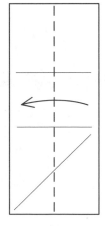

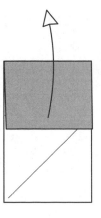

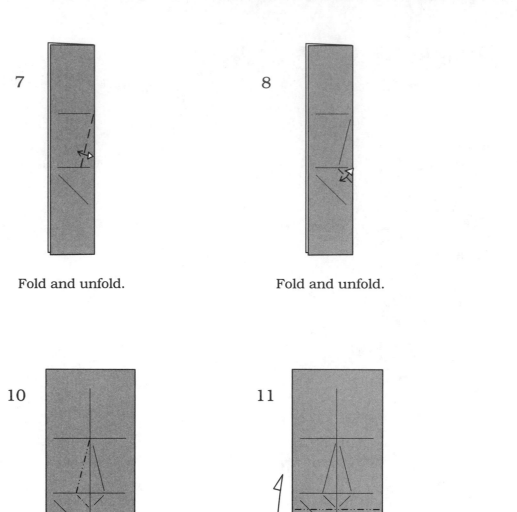

7

Fold and unfold.

8

Fold and unfold.

9

Unfold.

10

Fold and unfold to make
these mountain fold creases.

11

12

Lift up slightly on the
mountain fold line.

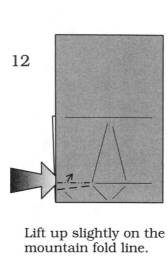

13

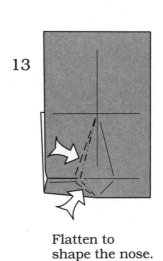

Flatten to
shape the nose.

14

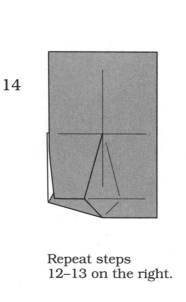

Repeat steps
12–13 on the right.

15

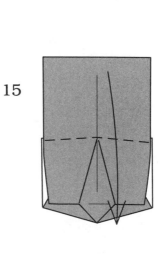

16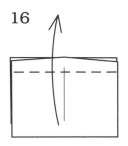

17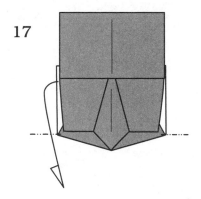

18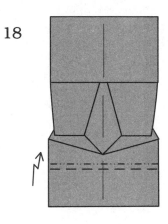

19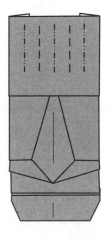

20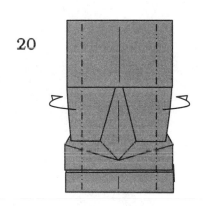

21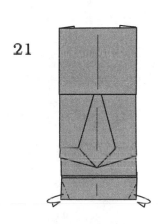

22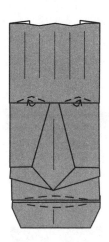

Fold and unfold.

23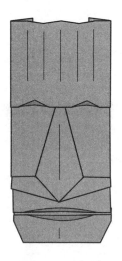

Shape the
eyes and lips.

24

African Mask

SHIRT WITH TIE

Designed by Stefan Delecat

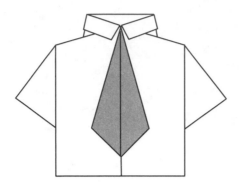

Begin with George
Washington on the front.

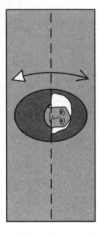

1

Fold and unfold.

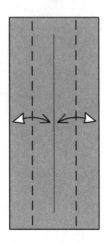

2

Fold and unfold.

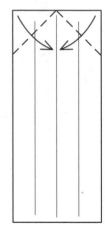

3

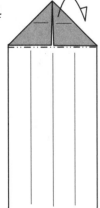

4

5

Unfold.

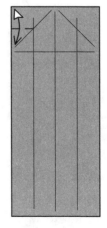

6

Fold and unfold.

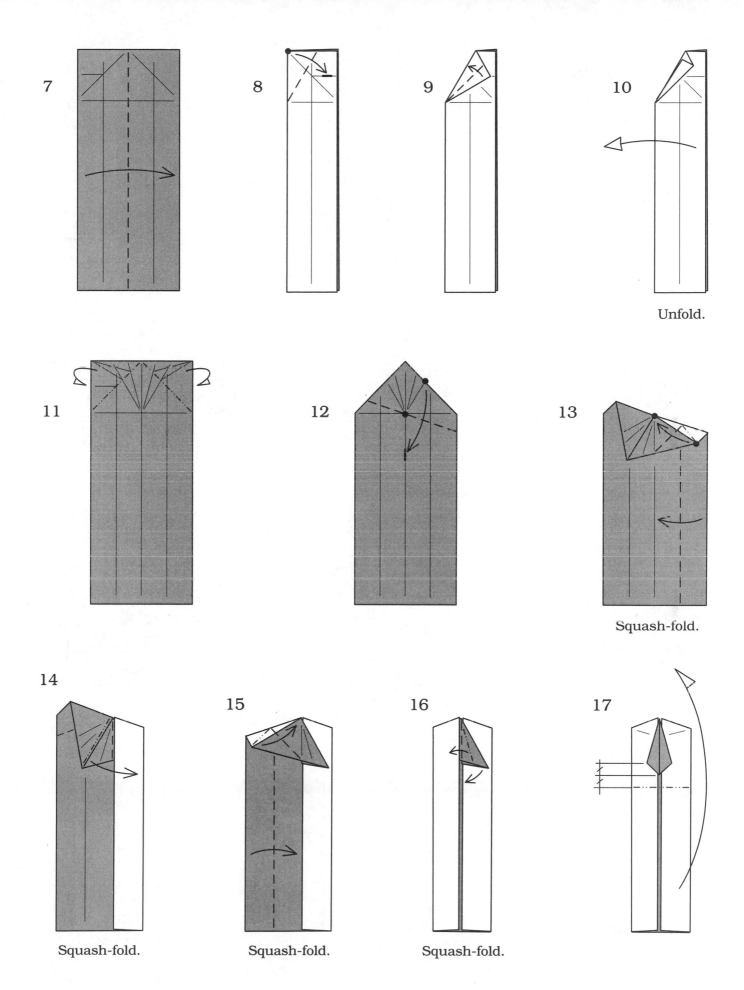

7

8

9

10

Unfold.

11

12

13

Squash-fold.

14

Squash-fold.

15

Squash-fold.

16

Squash-fold.

17

18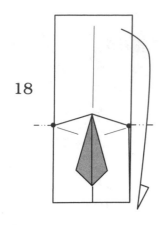

19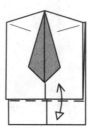

Fold and unfold.

20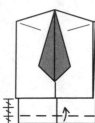

21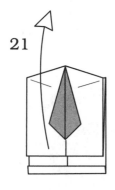

Lift up.

22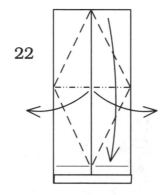

Mountain-fold along existing creases to form the sleeves.

23

Continue either with step 24 or go to step 28 for an alternative folding sequence to lock the back flap of the shirt.

24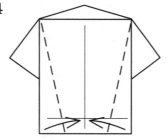

Fold the corners to the center line.

25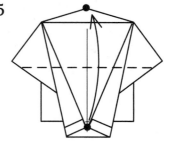

26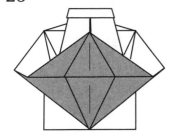

Bring the collar to the front.

27

Shirt with Tie (1)

28

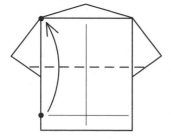

Fold the lower
part upward.

29

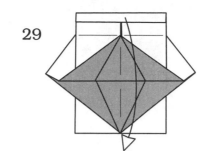

Unfold.

30

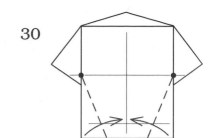

31

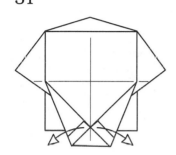

Unfold.

32

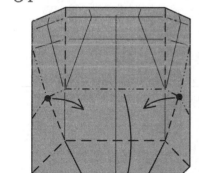

Unfold.

33

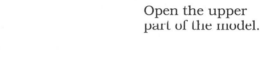

Open the upper
part of the model.

34

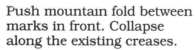

Push mountain fold between
marks in front. Collapse
along the existing creases.

35

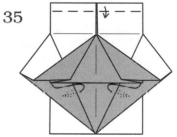

Put the corners
underneath and
refold the collar.

36

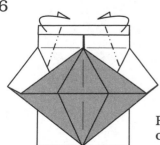

Refold and put the
collar on front.

37

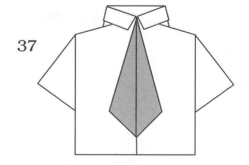

Shirt with Tie (2)

SWAN

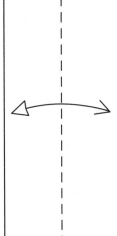

1

Fold and unfold.

2

3

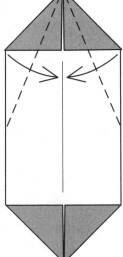

4

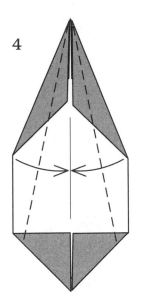

5

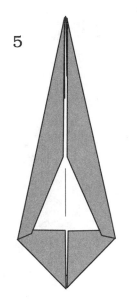

6

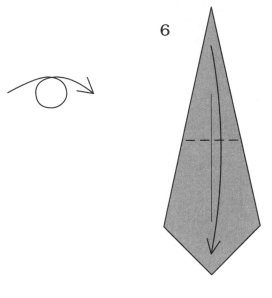

7

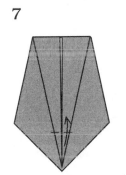

8

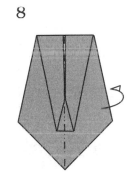

9

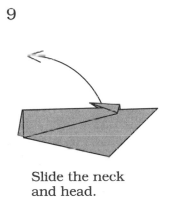

Slide the neck
and head.

10

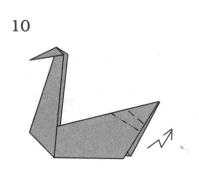

Crimp-fold the tail.

11

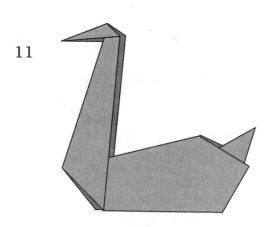

Swan

CRANE

1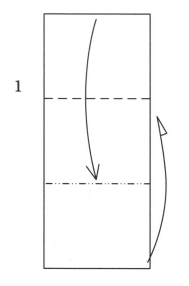

Fold in thirds.

2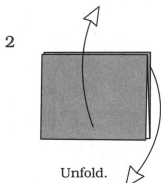

Unfold.

3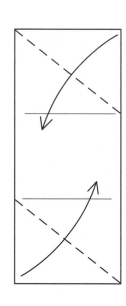

4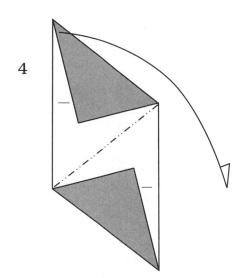

5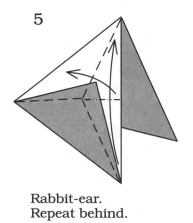

Rabbit-ear.
Repeat behind.

6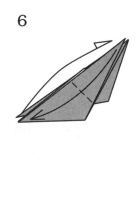

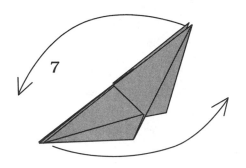

7

Rotate.

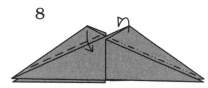

8

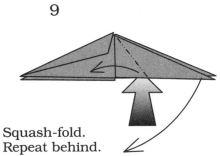

9

Squash-fold.
Repeat behind.

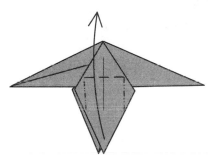

10

Petal-fold.
Repeat behind.

11

Double-rabbit ears.

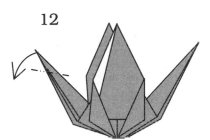

12

Reverse-fold.

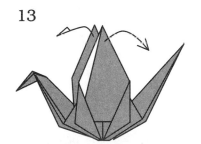

13

Spread the wings.

14

Crane

VULTURE

1

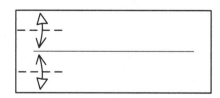

Fold and unfold.

2

Fold and unfold.

3

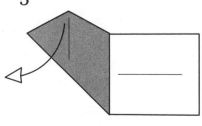

Bring the corners to the creases.

4

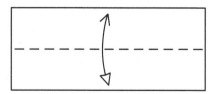

5

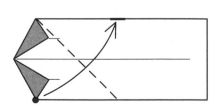

Unfold.

6

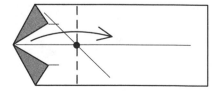

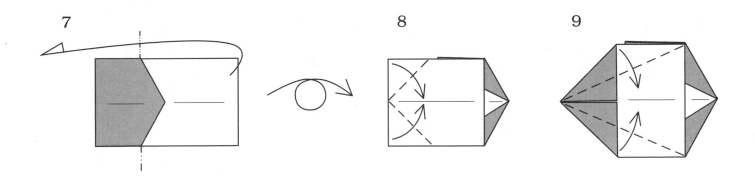

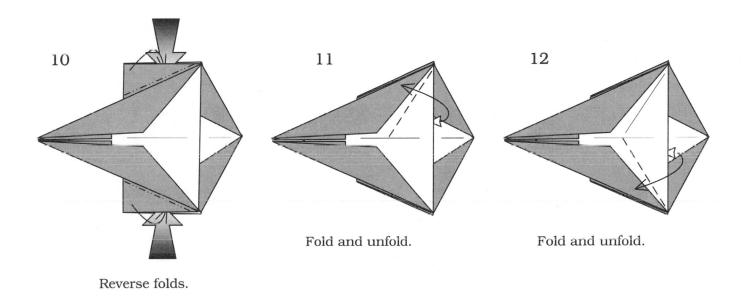

10

Reverse folds.

11

Fold and unfold.

12

Fold and unfold.

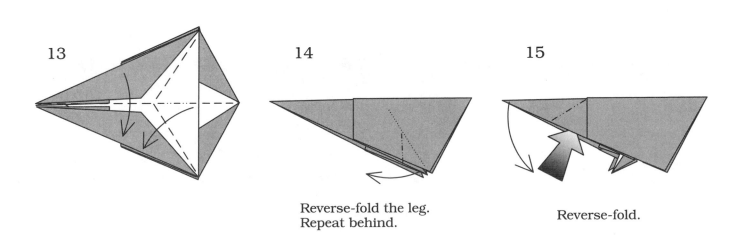

13

14

Reverse-fold the leg.
Repeat behind.

15

Reverse-fold.

16

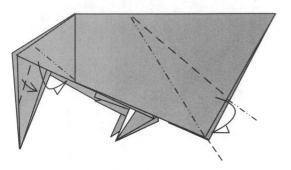

Fold inside at the neck
and repeat behind.
Crimp-fold the tail.

17

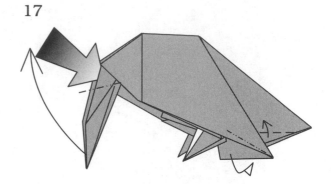

Reverse-fold the neck.
Push in by the wing and
tail. Repeat behind.

18

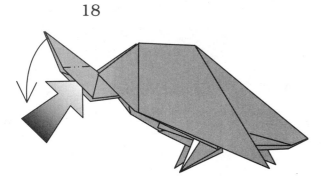

Reverse-fold.

19

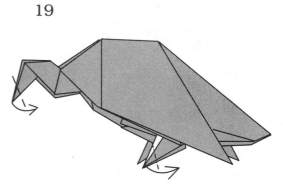

Outside-reverse-fold the
beak and reverse-fold
the feet. Repeat behind.

20

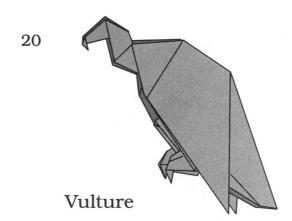

Vulture

GOOSE

1

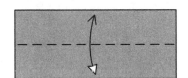

Fold and unfold.

2

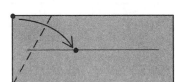

3

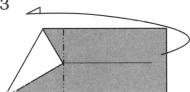

4

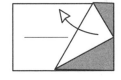

Unfold.

5

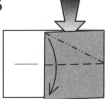

Squash-fold.

6

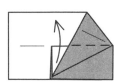

7

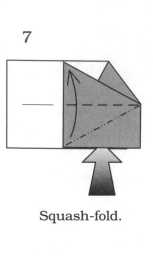

Squash-fold.

8

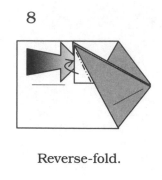

Reverse-fold.

9

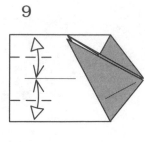

Fold and unfold.

10

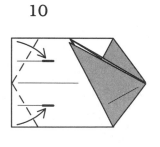

11

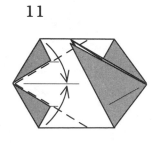

12

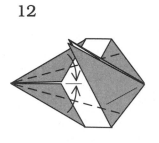

13

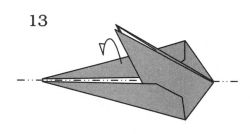

14

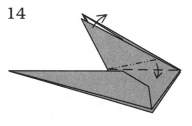

Crimp-fold.

15

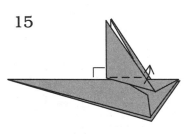

Note the right angle.
Repeat behind.

16

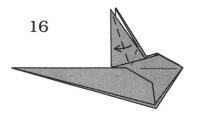

Squash-fold.
Repeat behind.

17

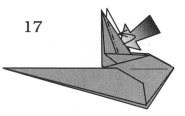

Reverse-fold.
Repeat behind.

18

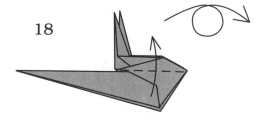

Repeat behind.

19

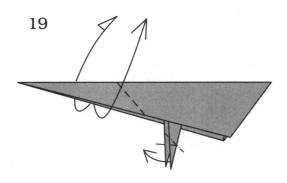

Outside-reverse-fold the
neck and crimp-fold the
feet. Repeat behind.

20

Outside-reverse-fold
and open the head.
Crimp-fold the tail.

21

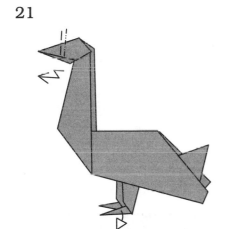

Crimp-fold the beak
and open the feet.
Repeat behind.

22

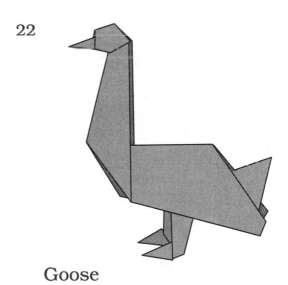

Goose

FLAMINGO

1

Fold and unfold.

2

3

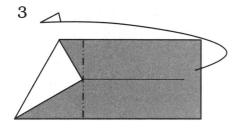

4

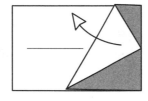

Unfold.

5

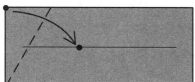

Squash-fold.

6

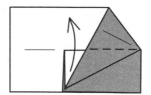

7

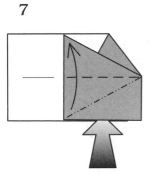

Squash-fold.

8

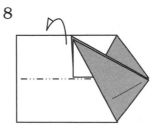

Reverse-fold.

9

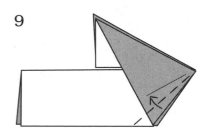

Repeat behind.

10

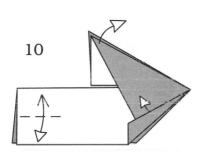

Unlock on the right
and fold and unfold
on the left.

11

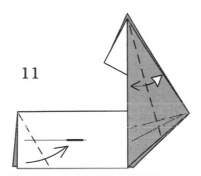

Fold and unfold all the
layers together on the right.
Repeat behind on the left.

12

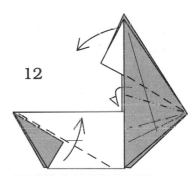

Crimp-fold on the right.
Repeat behind on the left.

13

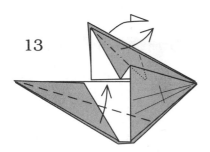

Crimp-fold at the top.
Repeat behind on the left.

14

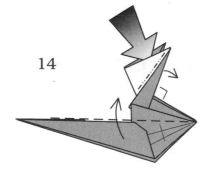

Note the right angle.
Reverse-fold at the top.
Repeat behind at the bottom.

15

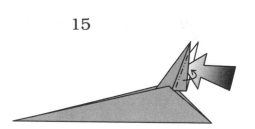

Reverse-fold
and rotate.

Flamingo 71

16

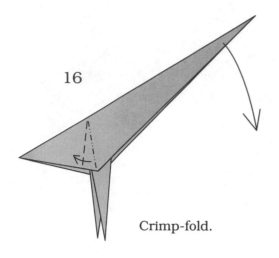

Crimp-fold.

17

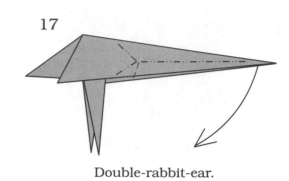

Double-rabbit-ear.

18

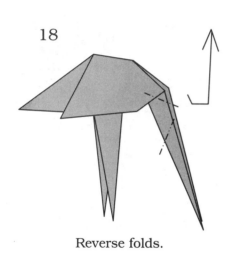

Reverse folds.

19

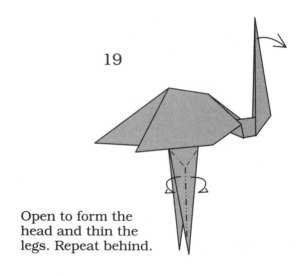

Open to form the
head and thin the
legs. Repeat behind.

20

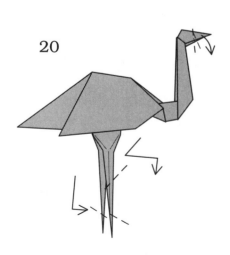

Crimp-fold the beak
and shape the legs.

21

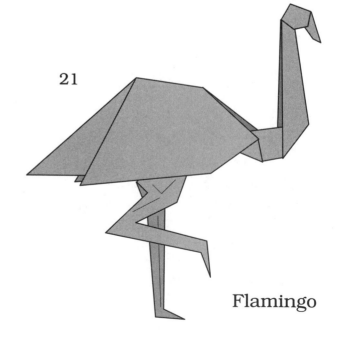

Flamingo

PEACOCK

Designed by Robert J. Lang

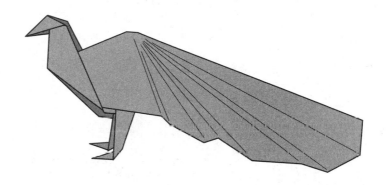

1

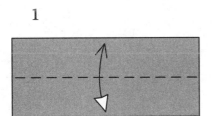

Fold and unfold.

2

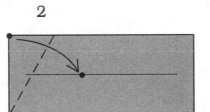

3

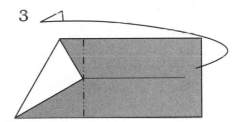

4

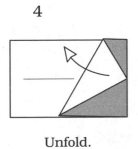

Unfold.

5

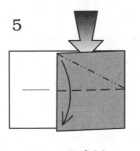

Squash-fold.

6

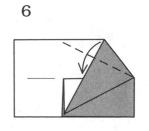

7

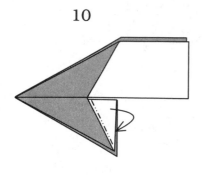

Squash-fold.

8

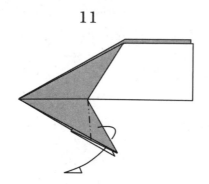

9

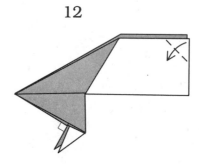

10

Reverse-fold.

11

Repeat behind.

12

Note the right angle by the legs. Repeat behind.

13

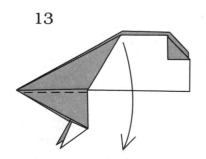

Repeat behind.

14

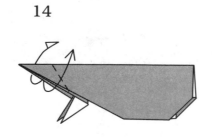

Outside-reverse-fold.

15

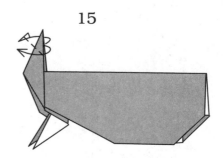

Outside-reverse-fold.

16

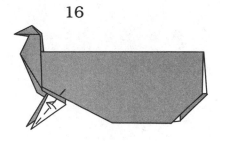

Repeat behind.

17

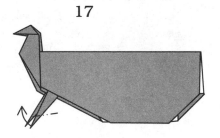

Reverse-fold.
Repeat behind.

18

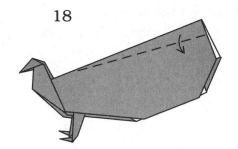

19

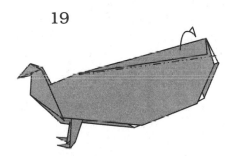

20

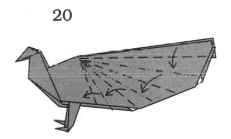

Continue folding
back and forth.

21

Open the
plumes.

22

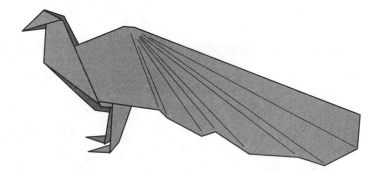

Peacock

PELICAN

1

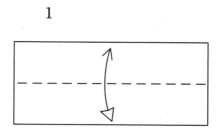

Fold and unfold.

2

Fold the corner to
the center edge.

3

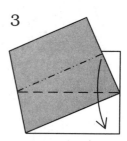

Squash-fold.

4

5

6

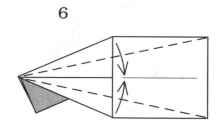

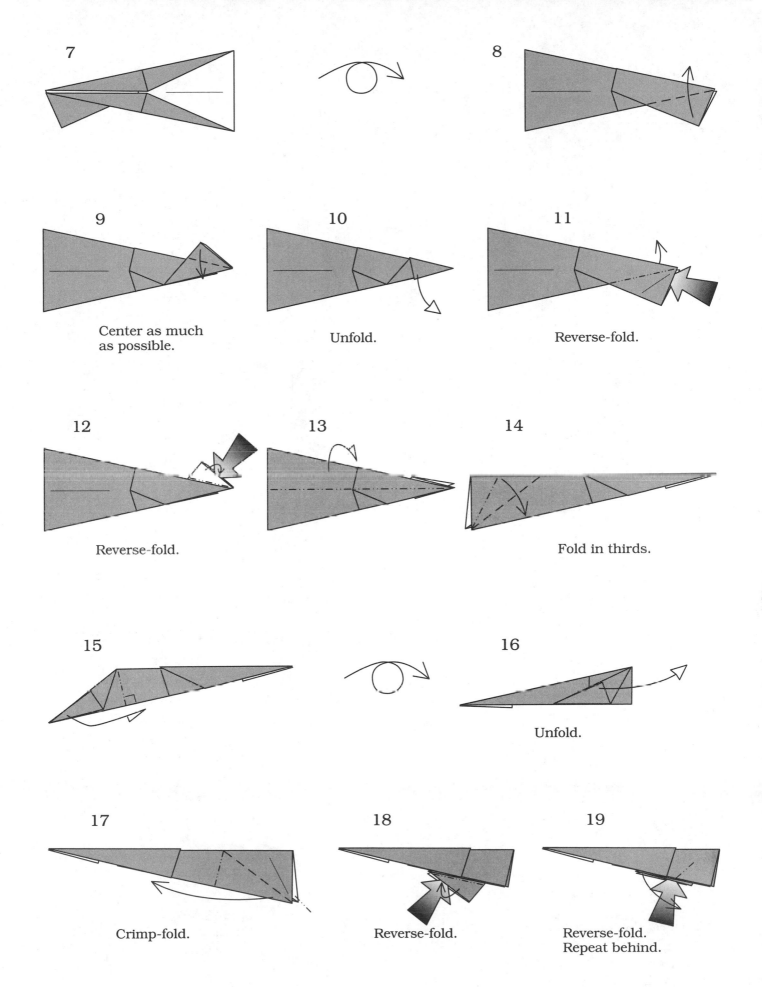

7

8

9

Center as much
as possible.

10

Unfold.

11

Reverse-fold.

12

Reverse-fold.

13

14

Fold in thirds.

15

16

Unfold.

17

Crimp-fold.

18

Reverse-fold.

19

Reverse-fold.
Repeat behind.

20

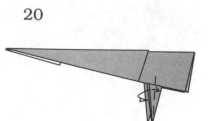

Fold front and back of the leg. Repeat behind.

21

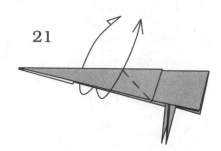

Outside-reverse-fold.

22

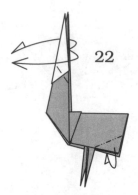

Outside-reverse-fold the head. Repeat behind at the back.

23

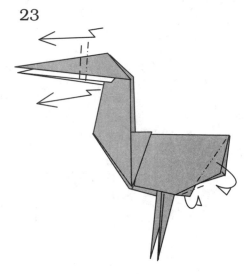

Crimp-fold the beak and lower the bottom one. Repeat behind at the back.

24

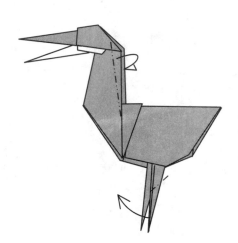

Reverse-fold the feet. Repeat behind.

25

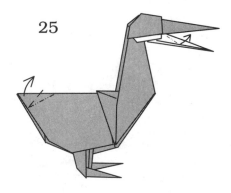

Crimp-fold the tail. Slide some paper at the beak.

26

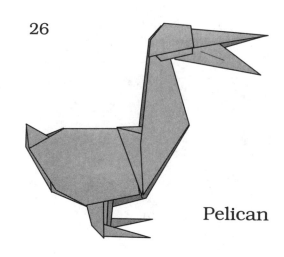

Pelican

EAGLE

Designed by Won Park

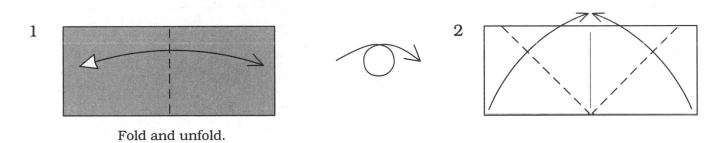

1

Fold and unfold.

2

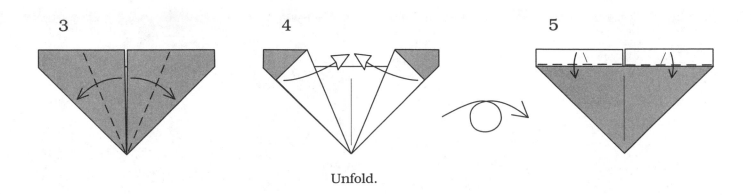

3

4

Unfold.

5

6

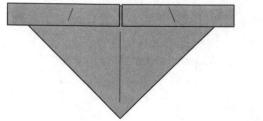

7

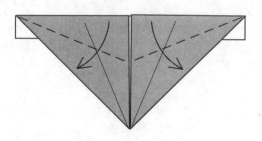

Unlock at the top.

8

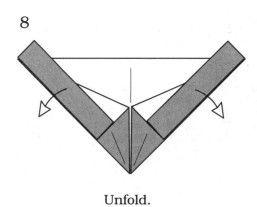

Unfold.

9

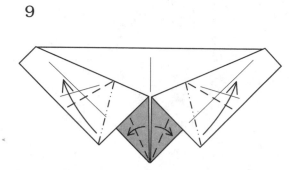

Squash folds.

10

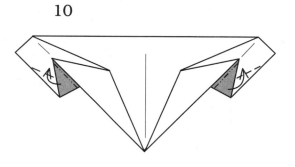

11

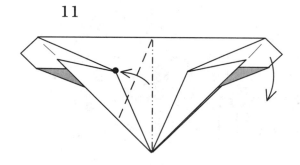

12

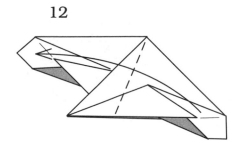

13

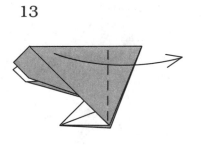

Repeat behind
and rotate.

14

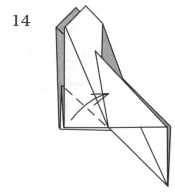

15

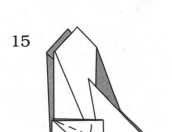

16

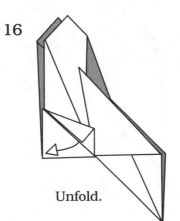

Unfold.

17

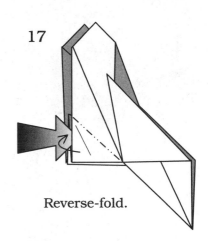

Reverse-fold.

18

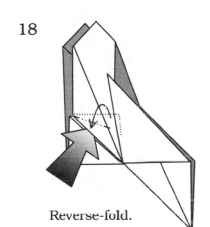

Reverse-fold.

19

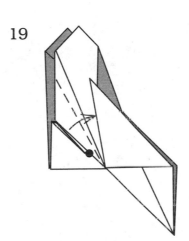

20

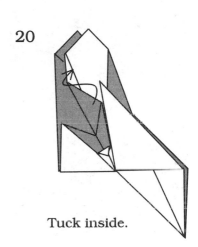

Tuck inside.

21

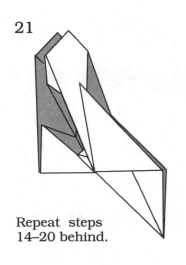

Repeat steps
14–20 behind.

22

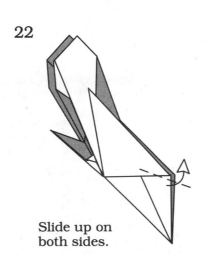

Slide up on
both sides.

23

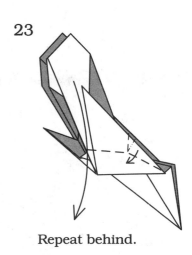

Repeat behind.

Eagle 81

24

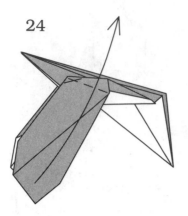

Fold the wings up but
keep the legs down.
Repeat behind.

25

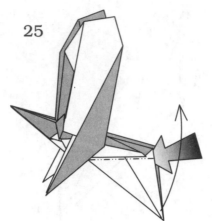

Reverse-fold.

26

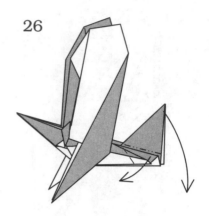

Crimp-fold.

27

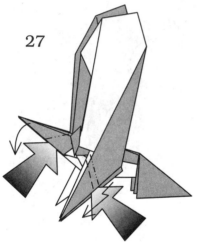

Crimp-fold the leg and
repeat behind.
Reverse-fold the head.

28

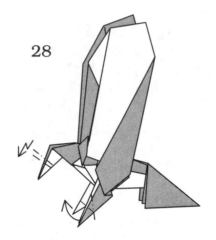

Crimp-fold the leg and
beak. Repeat behind.

29

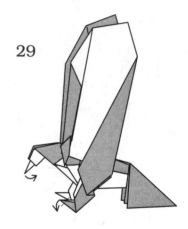

Reverse-fold the feet
and curl the beak.
Repeat behind.

30

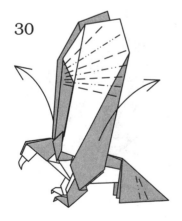

Fan the wings and tail.

31

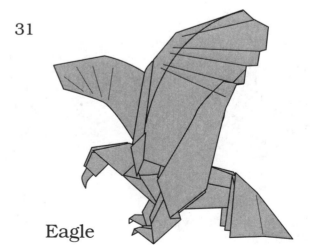

Eagle

ASIAN DRAGON

Designed by Gay Merrill Gross

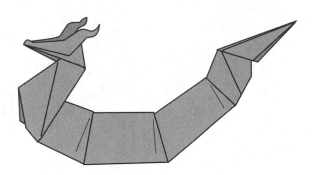

1

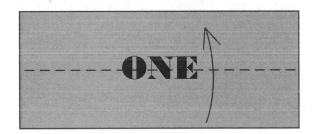

Begin with the "ONE" on the front.

2

Repeat behind.

3

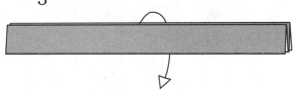

Unfold from behind.

4

Fold and unfold on the left.

5

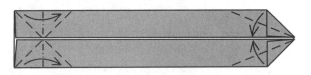

Collapse into a Waterbomb
Base on the left.

6

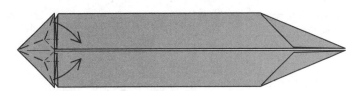

Fold two rabbit ears on the left.

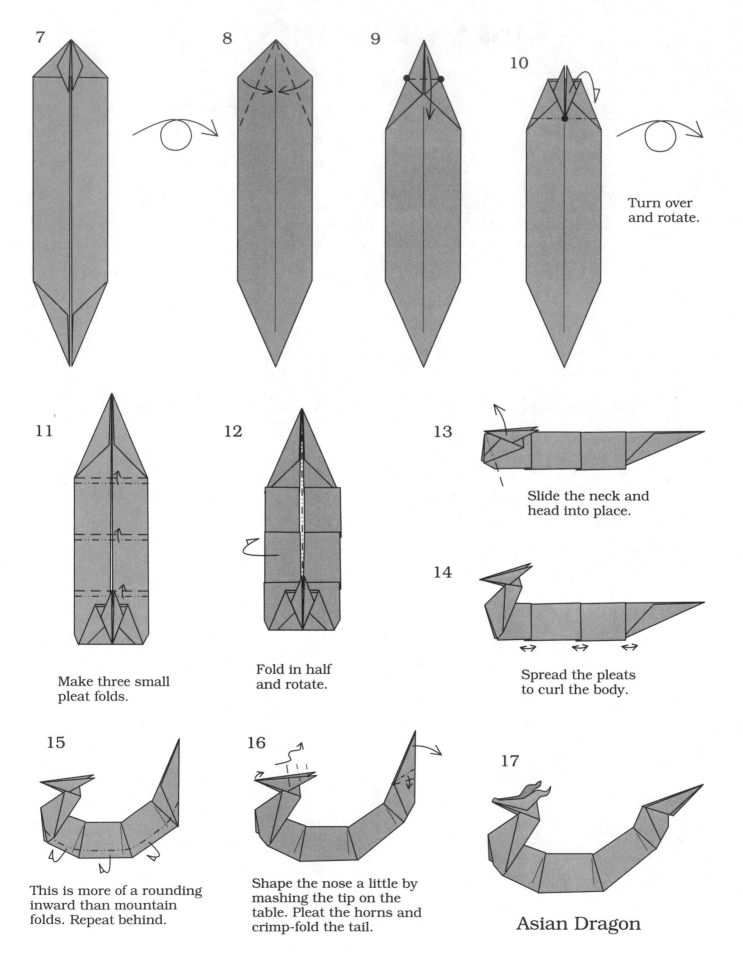

7

8

9

10

Turn over
and rotate.

11

Make three small
pleat folds.

12

Fold in half
and rotate.

13

Slide the neck and
head into place.

14

Spread the pleats
to curl the body.

15

This is more of a rounding
inward than mountain
folds. Repeat behind.

16

Shape the nose a little by
mashing the tip on the
table. Pleat the horns and
crimp-fold the tail.

17

Asian Dragon

ALLIGATOR

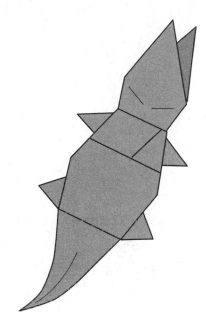

1

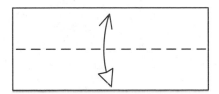

Fold and unfold.

2

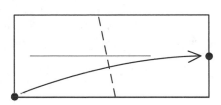

Fold the corner to
the center edge.

3

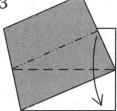

Squash-fold.

4

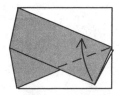

Center as much
as possible.

5

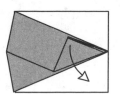

Unfold.

6

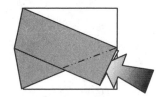

Reverse-fold.

7

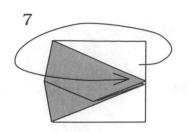

Wrap the paper in back
all the way to the front.

8

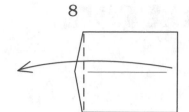

9

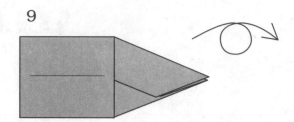

10

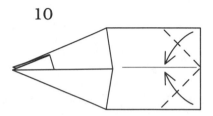

11

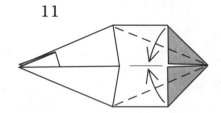

12

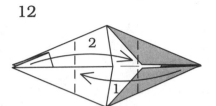

Divide in thirds.

13

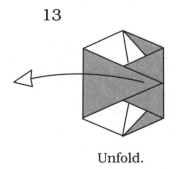

Unfold.

14

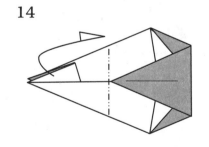

15

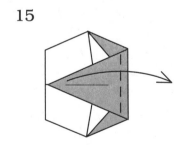

16

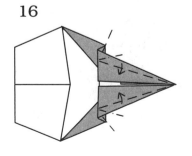

Make thin squash folds.

17

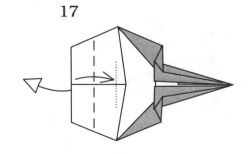

18

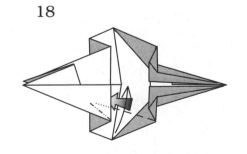

Fold inside and rotate.

19

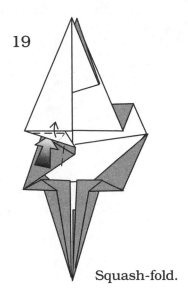

Squash-fold.

20

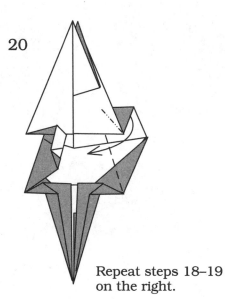

Repeat steps 18–19 on the right.

21

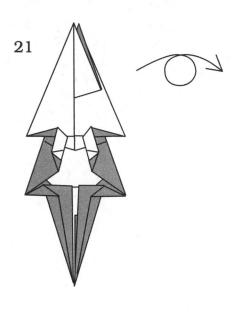

22

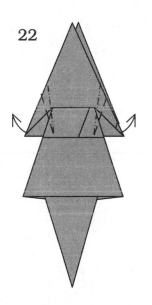

Pleat the front legs.

23

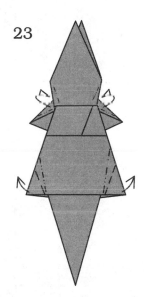

Squash-fold the front legs and pleat the hind legs.

24

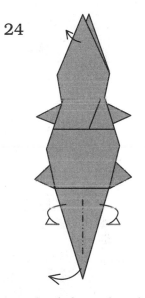

Curl the tail and open the head.

25

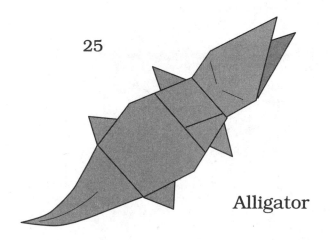

Alligator

TYRANNOSAURUS

1

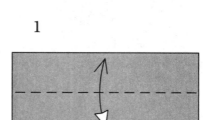

Fold and unfold.

2

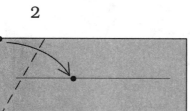

3

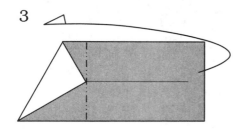

4

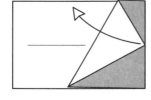

Unfold.

5

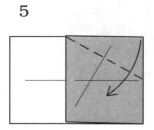

6

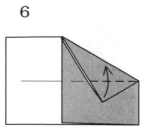

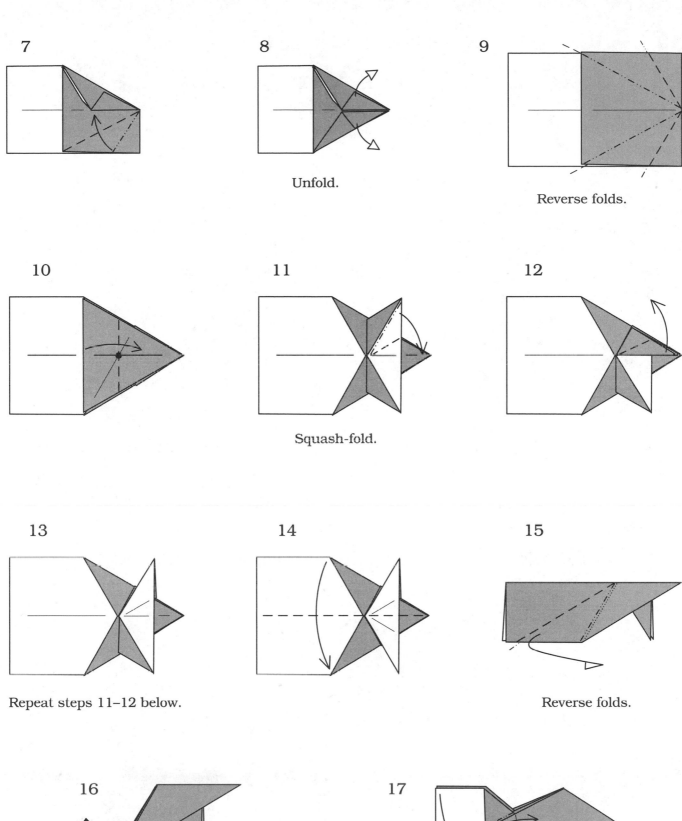

7

8

Unfold.

9

Reverse folds.

10

11

Squash-fold.

12

13

Repeat steps 11–12 below.

14

15

Reverse folds.

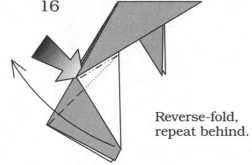

16

Reverse-fold,
repeat behind.

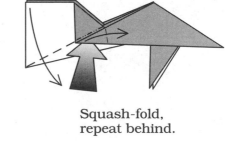

17

Squash-fold,
repeat behind.

18

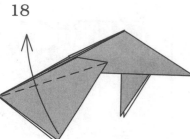

Repeat behind.

19

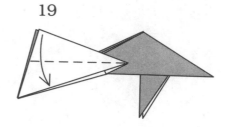

Repeat behind.

20

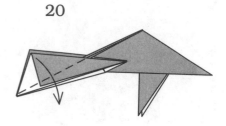

Repeat behind.

21

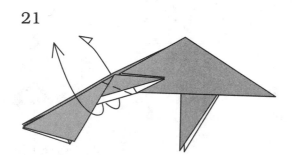

Outside-reverse-fold.

22

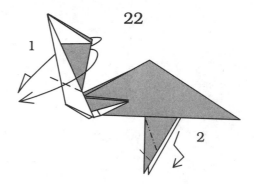

1. Outside-reverse-fold.
2. Reverse folds.
Repeat behind.

23

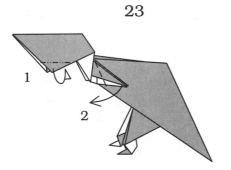

Repeat behind.

25

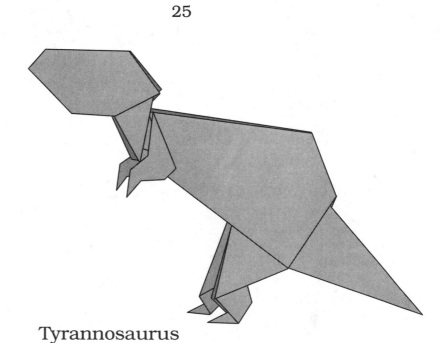

24

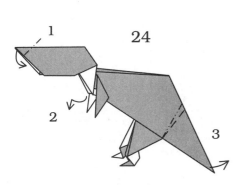

1. Reverse-fold.
2. Shape the arms.
3. Crimp-fold.

Tyrannosaurus

RABBIT

Designed by Peter Farina

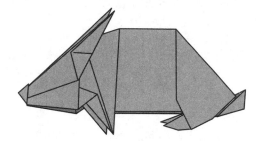

1

Fold and unfold. Turn over and rotate.

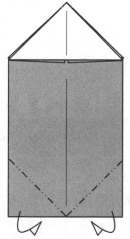

2

Fold and unfold.

3

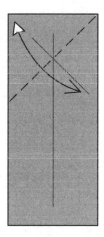

Fold and unfold.

4

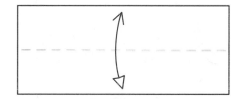

5

6

7

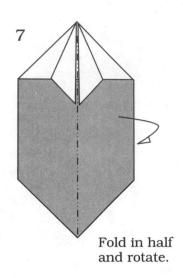

Fold in half
and rotate.

8

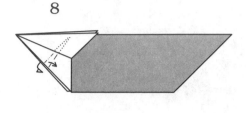

Crimp-fold.

9

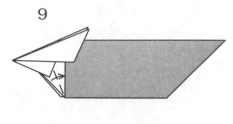

Repeat behind.

10

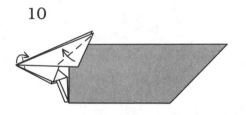

Outside-reverse-fold the nose.
Repeat behind for the ears.

11

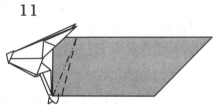

Crimp-fold.

12

Squash-fold.
Repeat behind.

13

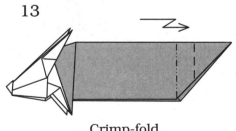
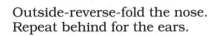

Crimp-fold.

14

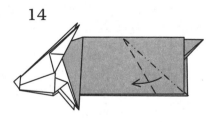

Crimp-fold.

15

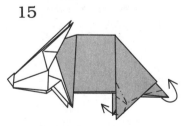

Crimp-fold the legs and
outside-reverse-fold the tail.
Repeat behind. To finish the
model open the tail, open
and shape the ears, open
and shape the body.

16

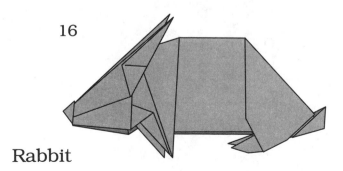

Rabbit

ARMADILLO

Desinged by Jim Cowling

1

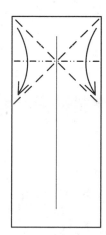

Fold and unfold. Rotate.

2

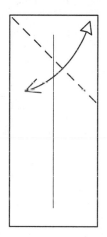

Fold and unfold.

3

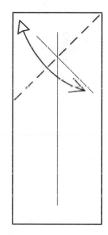

Fold and unfold.

4

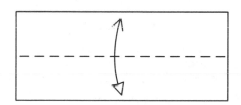

5

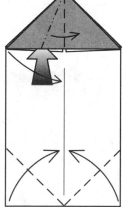

Squash-fold the ear.

6

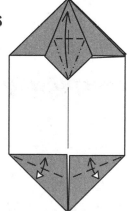

Petal-fold the ear. Fold
and unfold by the tail.

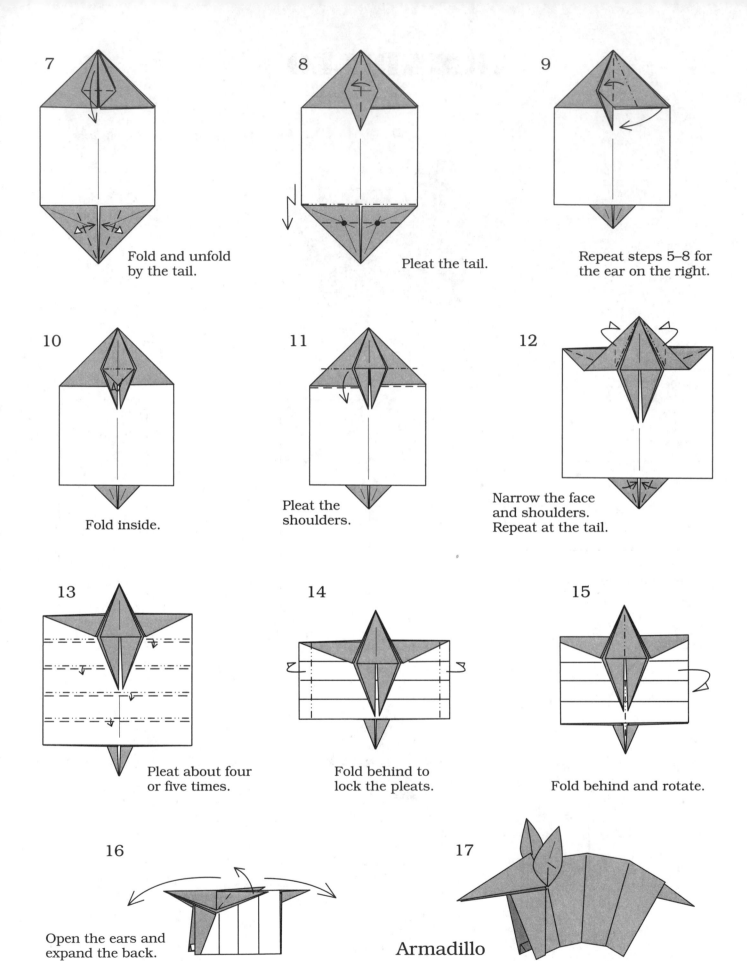

7 Fold and unfold by the tail.

8 Pleat the tail.

9 Repeat steps 5–8 for the ear on the right.

10 Fold inside.

11 Pleat the shoulders.

12 Narrow the face and shoulders. Repeat at the tail.

13 Pleat about four or five times.

14 Fold behind to lock the pleats.

15 Fold behind and rotate.

16 Open the ears and expand the back.

17 Armadillo

SQUIRREL

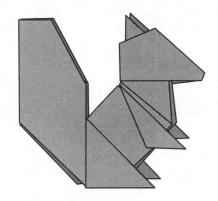

1

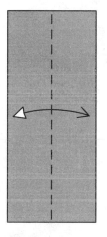

Fold and unfold.

2

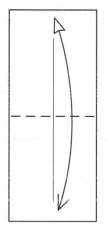

Fold and unfold.

3

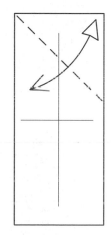

Fold and unfold.

4

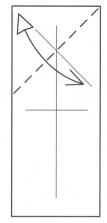

Fold and unfold.

5

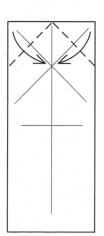

6

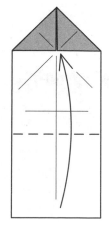

7

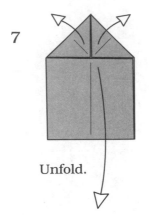

Unfold.

8

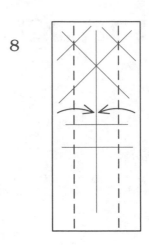

9

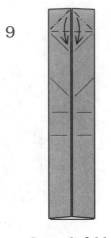

Squash folds.

10

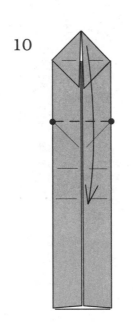

11

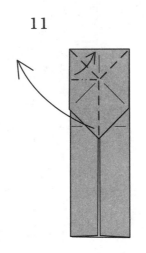

Rabbit-ear.

12

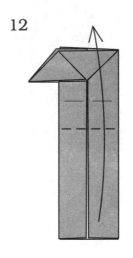

13

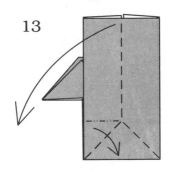

Rabbit-ear.

14

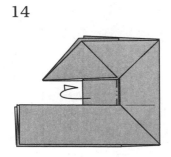

15

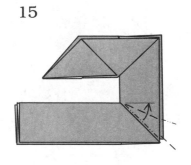

Crimp-fold.

16

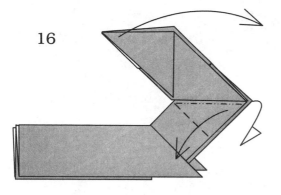

Crimp-fold.

17

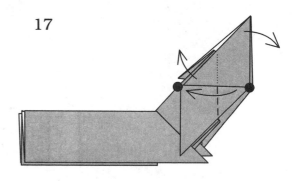

Crimp-fold.

18

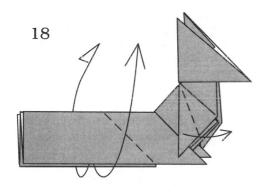

Outside-reverse-fold the tail.
Repeat behind for the arms.

19

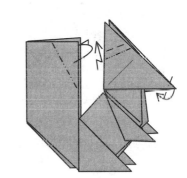

Pleat-fold the ears,
reverse-fold the face.
Repeat behind.

20

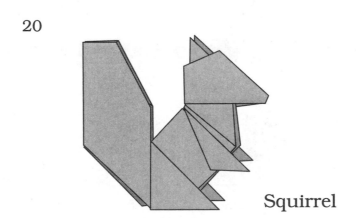

Squirrel

AARDVARK

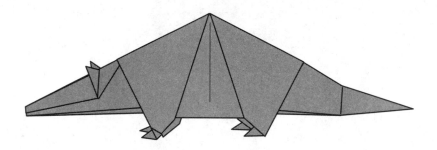

1

Fold and unfold.

2

3

4

5

Unfold.

6

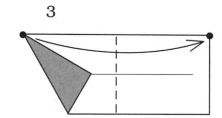

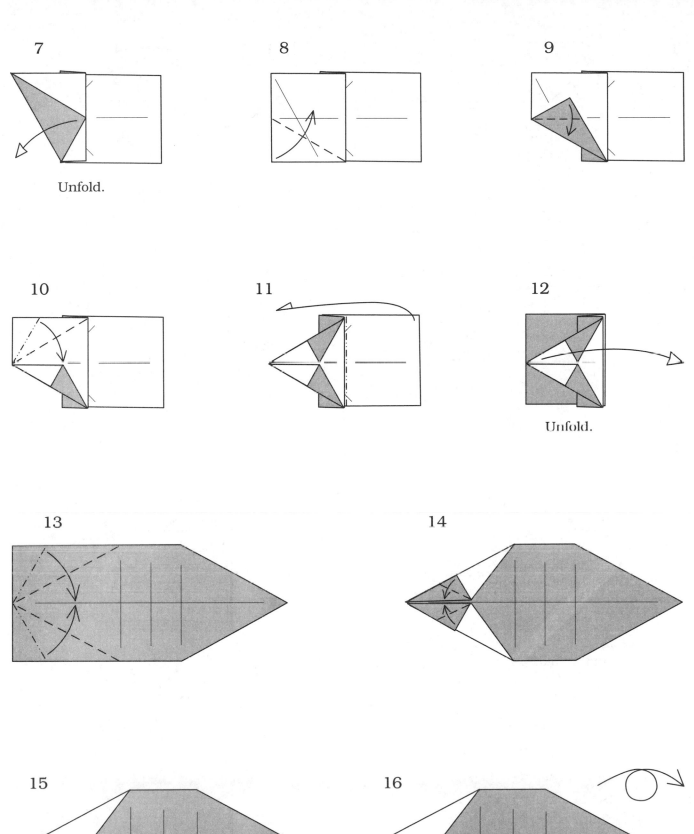

7

Unfold.

8

9

10

11

12

Unfold.

13

14

15

Squash folds.

16

17

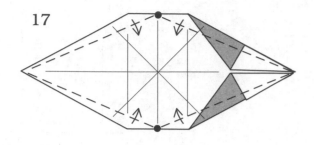

18

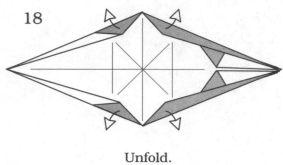

Unfold.

19

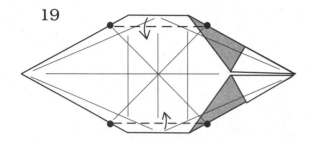

20

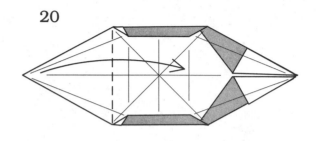

21

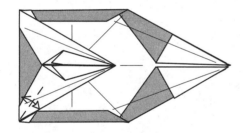

Fold and unfold.

22

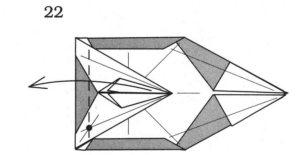

23

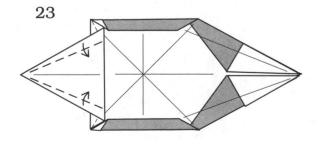

Squash folds.

24

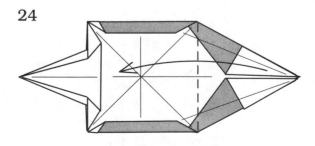

Repeat steps 20–23
on the right.

25

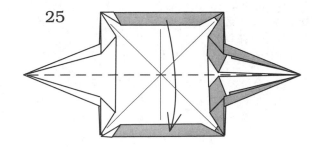

26

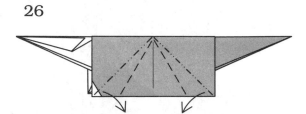

Repeat behind.

27

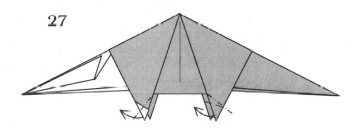

Reverse-fold the front legs
and crimp-fold the hind
legs. Repeat behind.

28

Crimp-fold the tail,
reverse-fold the head, and
repeat behind at the ears.

29

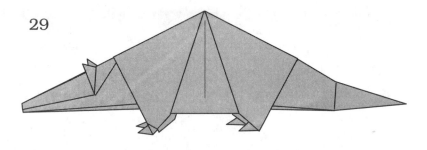

Aardvark

LLAMA

1

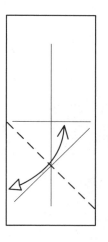

Fold and unfold. Rotate.

2

Fold and unfold.

3

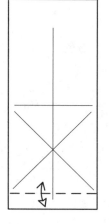

4

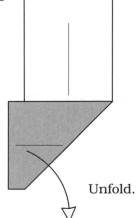

Unfold.

5

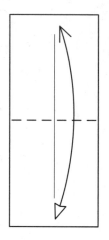

Fold and unfold.

6

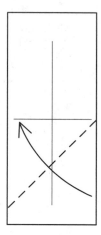

Fold and unfold.

7

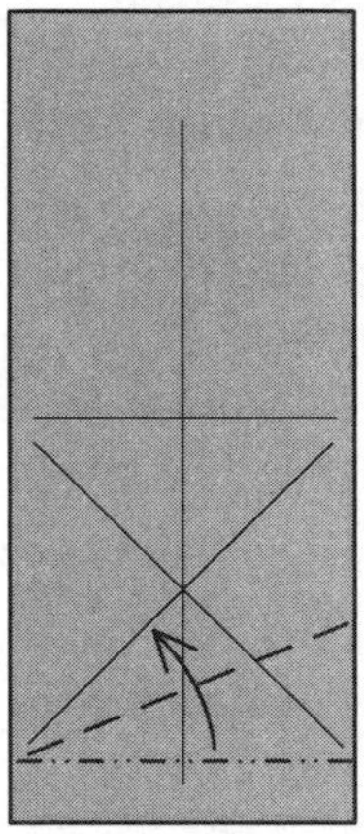

8

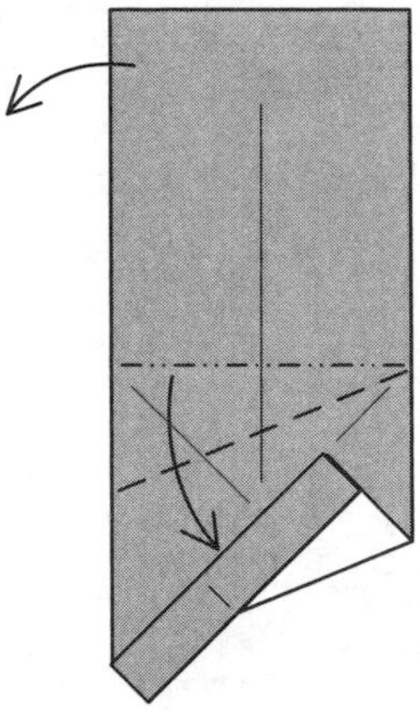

9

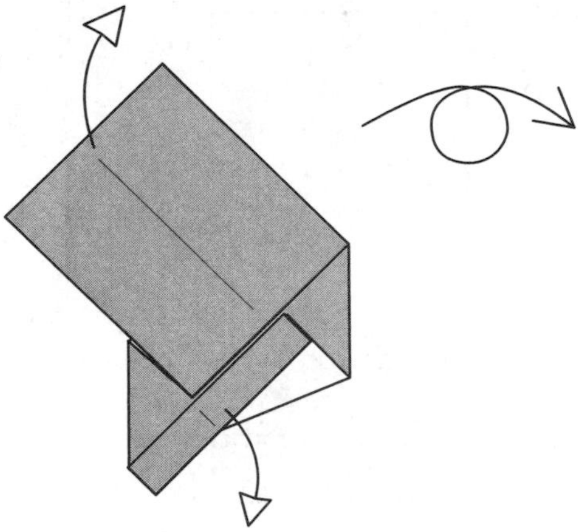

Unfold.

10

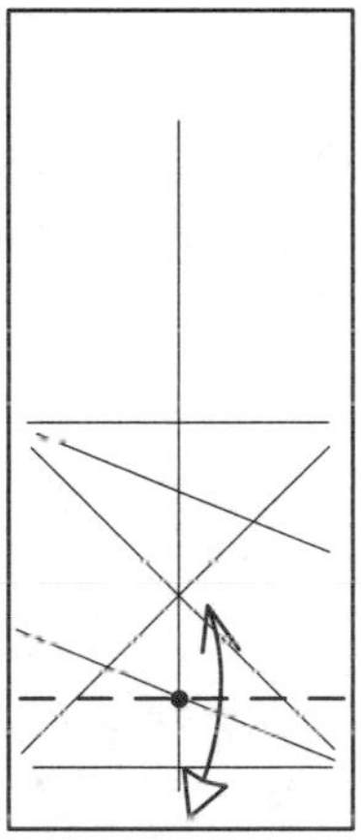

Fold and unfold.

11

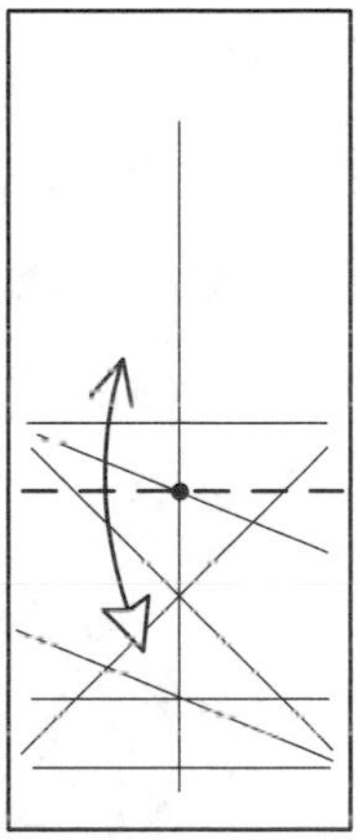

Fold and unfold.

12

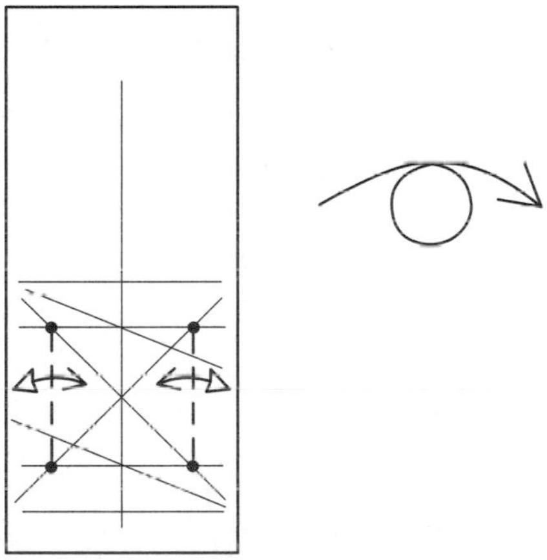

Fold and unfold.

13

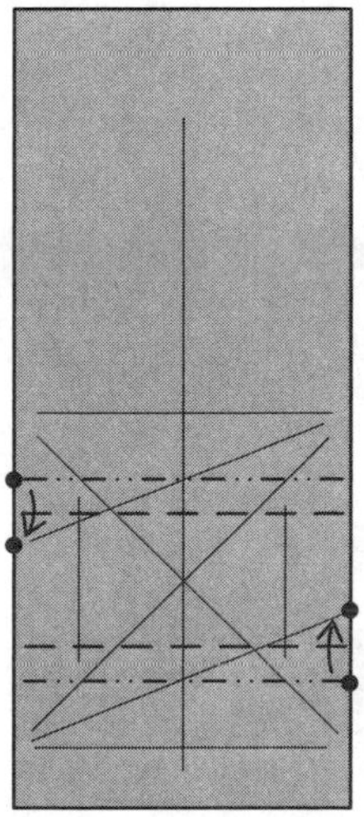

14

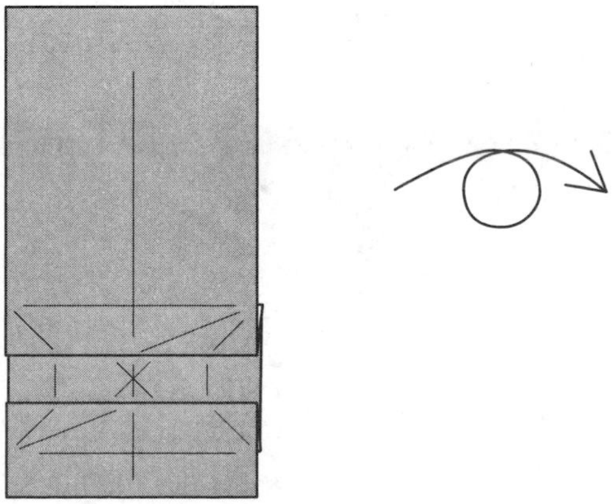

15

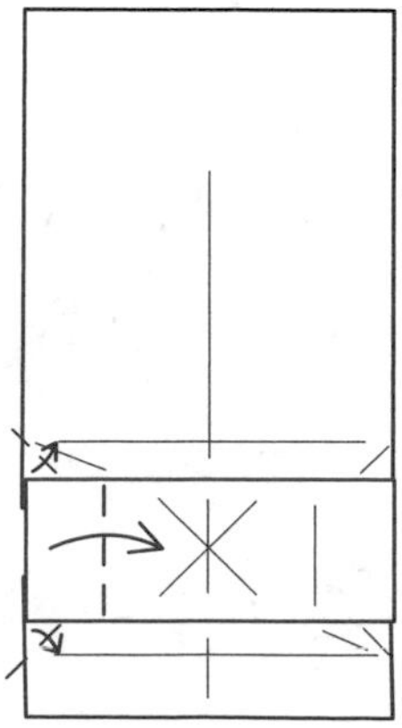

Llama 103

16

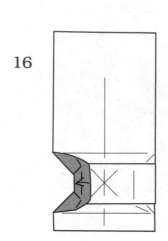

Flatten.

17

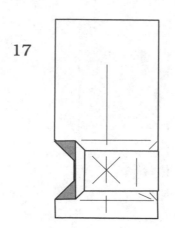

Repeat steps 15–16
on the right.

18

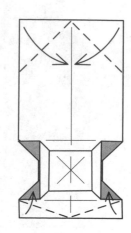

19

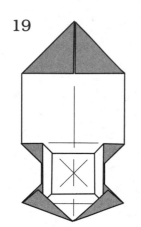

20

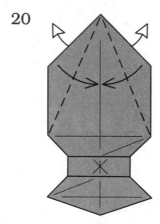

21

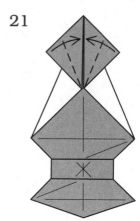

22

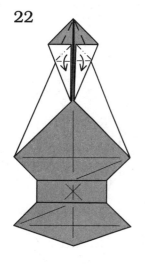

Squash folds.

23

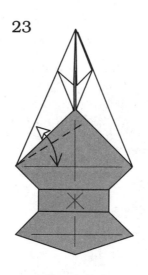

Fold and unfold.

24

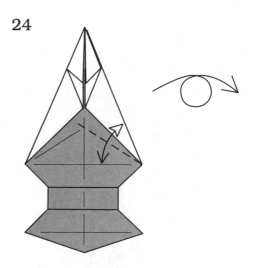

Fold and unfold.

25

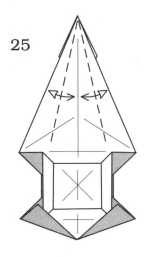

Fold and unfold.

26

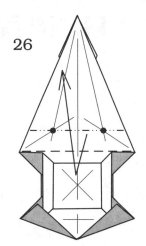

27

Squash folds.

28

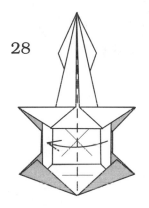

Fold in half and rotate.

29

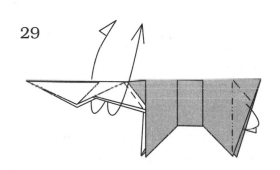

Outside-reverse-fold the
neck and crimp-fold the tail.

30

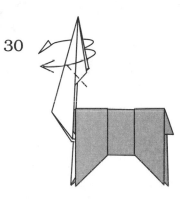

Outside-reverse-fold.

31

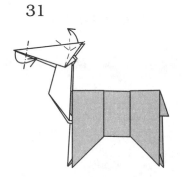

Rabbit-ear the ear and
repeat behind.
Reverse-fold the head.

32

Crimp-fold the
head. Thin the legs
and repeat behind.

33

Llama

BISON

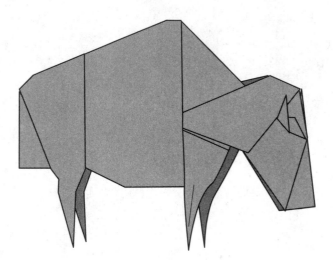

1

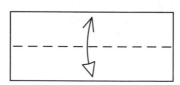

Fold and unfold.

2

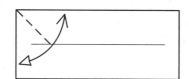

Fold and unfold.

3

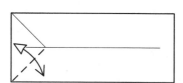

Fold and unfold.

4

Fold and unfold.

5

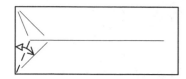

Fold and unfold.

6

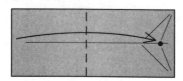

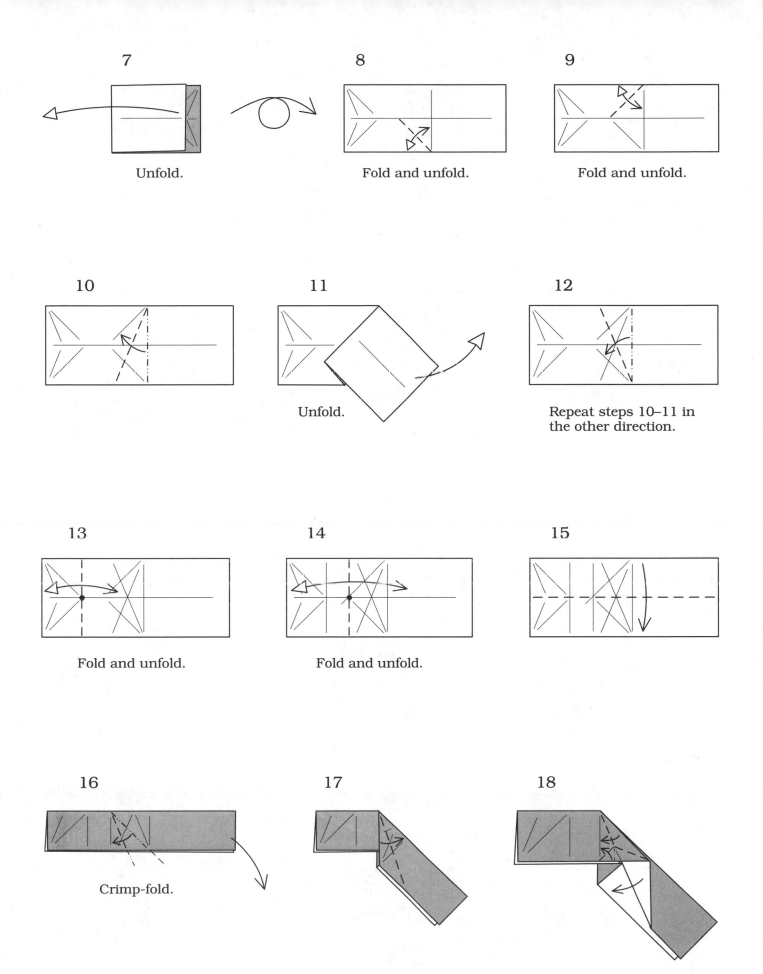

7

Unfold.

8

Fold and unfold.

9

Fold and unfold.

10

11

Unfold.

12

Repeat steps 10–11 in the other direction.

13

Fold and unfold.

14

Fold and unfold.

15

16

Crimp-fold.

17

18

Bison 107

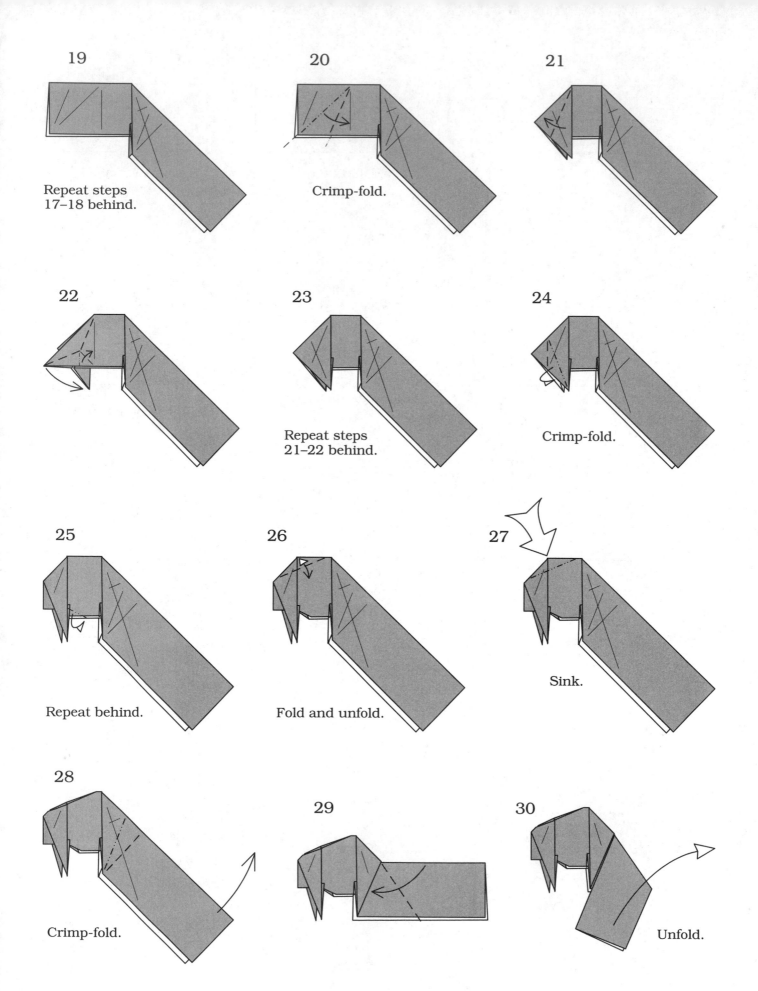

19

Repeat steps
17–18 behind.

20

Crimp-fold.

21

22

23

Repeat steps
21–22 behind.

24

Crimp-fold.

25

Repeat behind.

26

Fold and unfold.

27

Sink.

28

Crimp-fold.

29

30

Unfold.

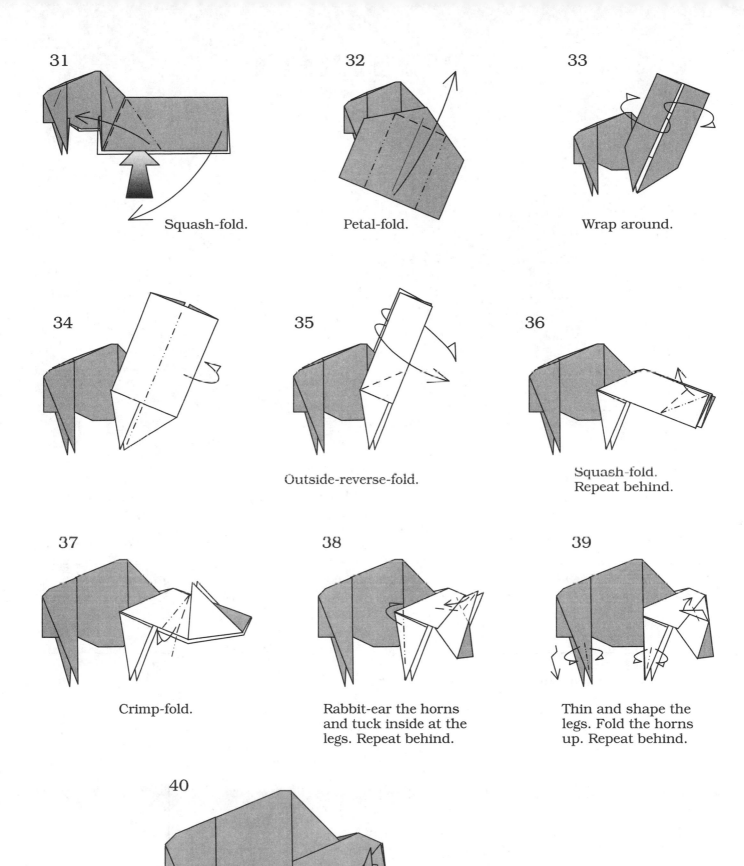

31

Squash-fold.

32

Petal-fold.

33

Wrap around.

34

35

Outside-reverse-fold.

36

Squash-fold.
Repeat behind.

37

Crimp-fold.

38

Rabbit-ear the horns
and tuck inside at the
legs. Repeat behind.

39

Thin and shape the
legs. Fold the horns
up. Repeat behind.

40

Bison

BUTTERFLY

Designed by Won Park

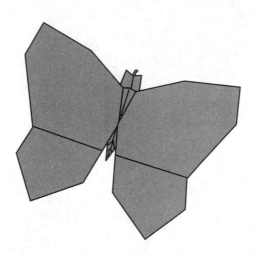

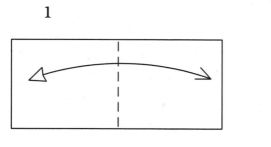

1

Fold and unfold.

2

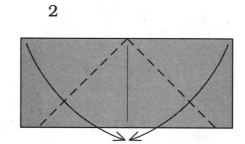

3

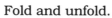

4

5

Unfold, turn
over, and rotate.

6

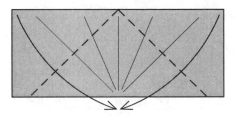

Repeat steps 2–5.

7

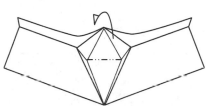

Fold and unfold.

8

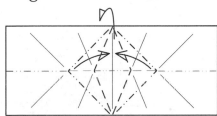

9

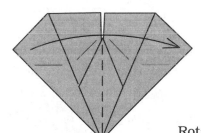

This is a three-dimensional
intermediate step.

10

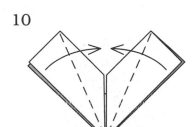

11

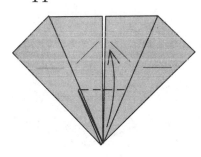

12

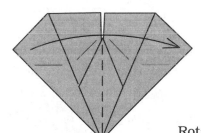

Rotate.

13

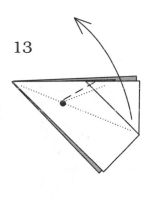

14

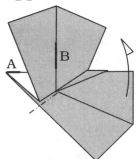

Note that lines A and B
form a right angle.

15

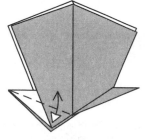

Fold and unfold.
Repeat behind.

16

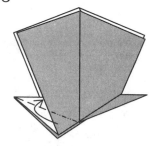

Reverse-fold.
Repeat behind.

17

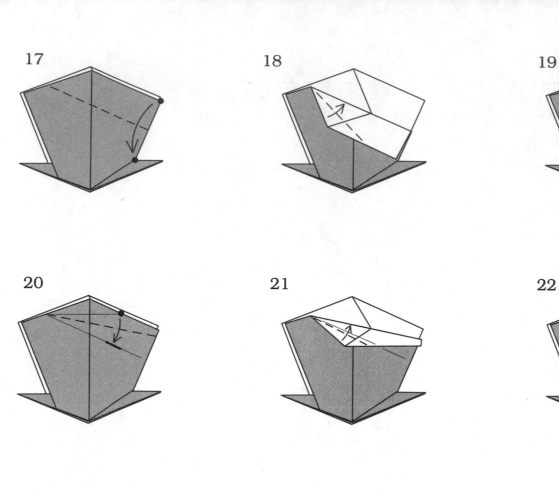

18

19

Unfold.

20

21

22

Unfold.

23

Pull apart.

24

Flatten.

25

Repeat steps
17-24 behind.

26

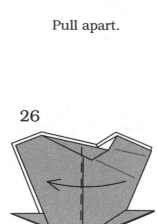

Repeat behind.

27

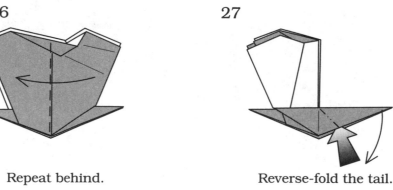

Reverse-fold the tail.

28

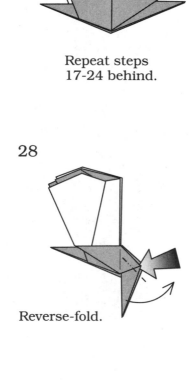

Reverse-fold.

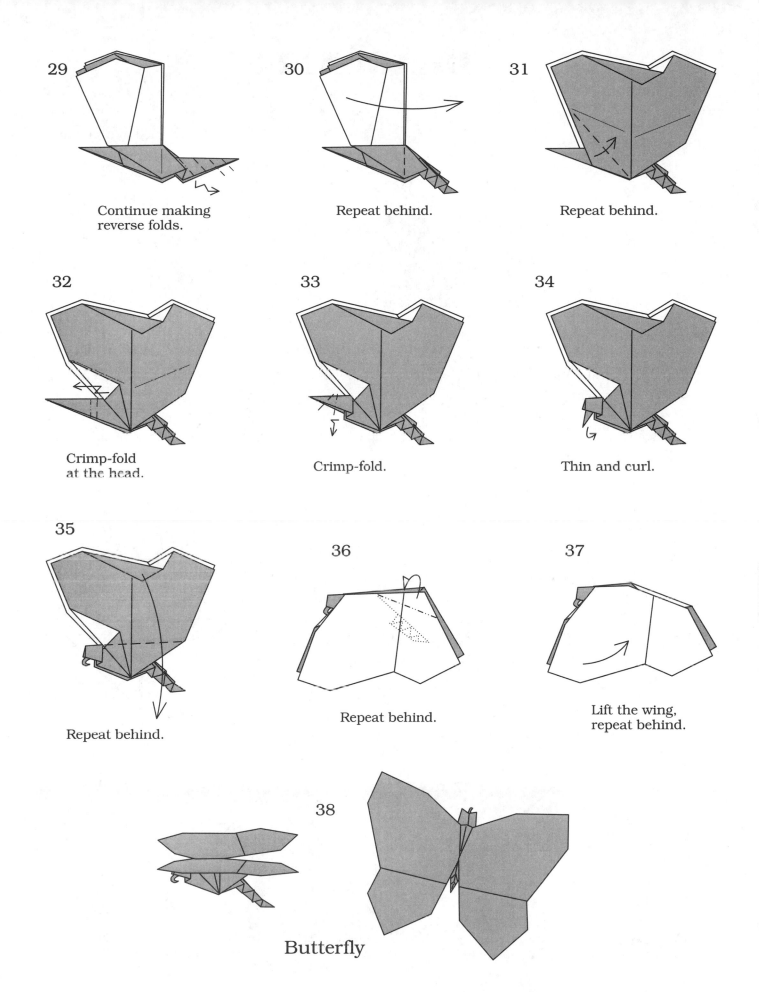

29 Continue making reverse folds.

30 Repeat behind.

31 Repeat behind.

32 Crimp-fold at the head.

33 Crimp-fold.

34 Thin and curl.

35 Repeat behind.

36 Repeat behind.

37 Lift the wing, repeat behind.

38

Butterfly

DRAGONFLY

Designed by Won Park

Begin with step 10
of the butterfly.

1

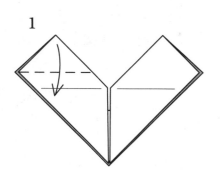

2

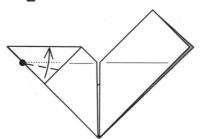

3

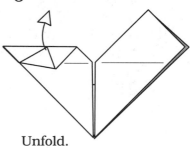

Unfold.

4

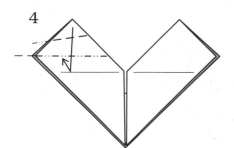

Make two reverse folds
along the creases.

5

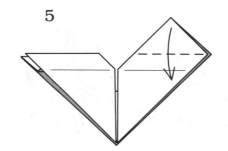

Repeat steps 1–4
on the right.

6

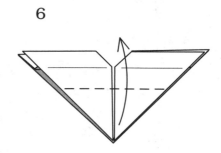

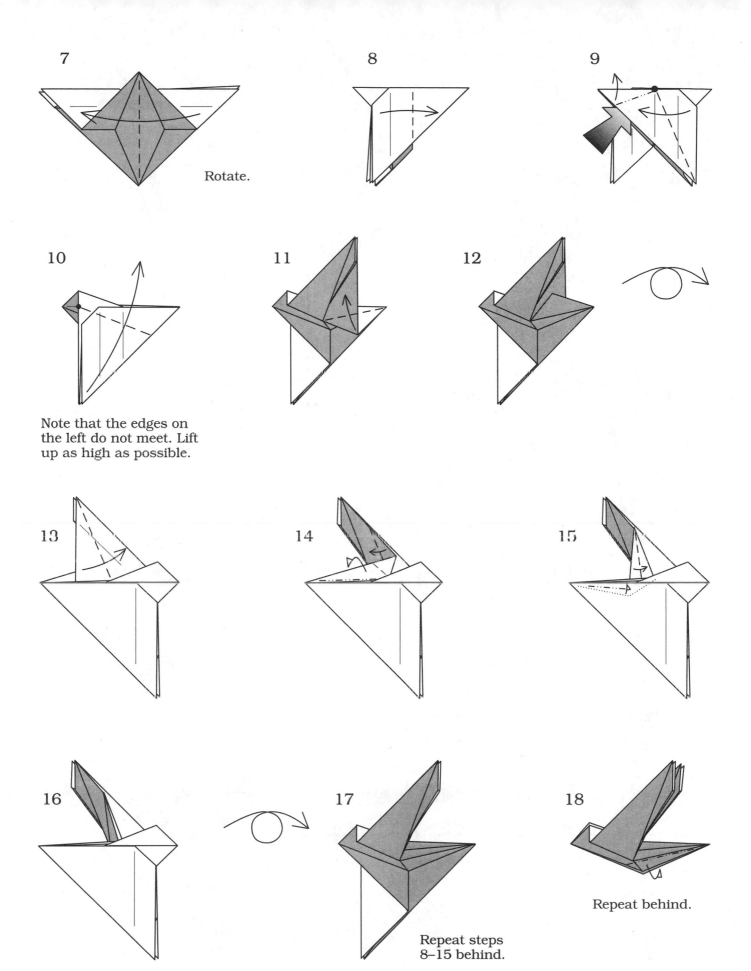

7

Rotate.

8

9

10

Note that the edges on the left do not meet. Lift up as high as possible.

11

12

13

14

15

16

17

Repeat steps 8–15 behind.

18

Repeat behind.

Dragonfly 115

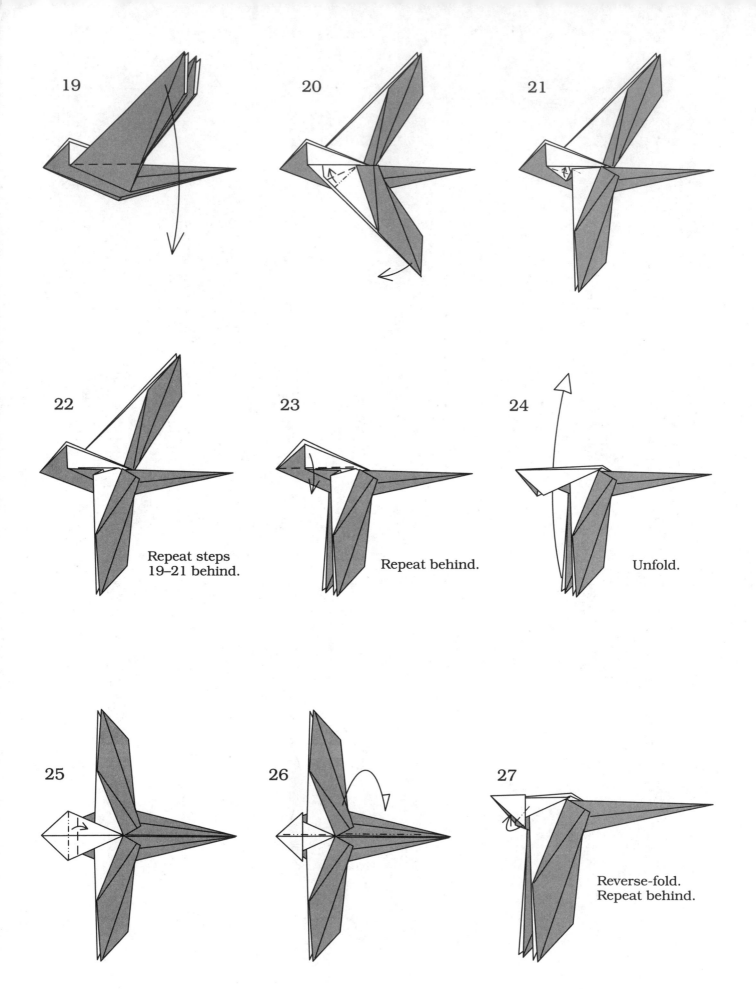

19

20

21

22

Repeat steps
19–21 behind.

23

Repeat behind.

24

Unfold.

25

26

27

Reverse-fold.
Repeat behind.

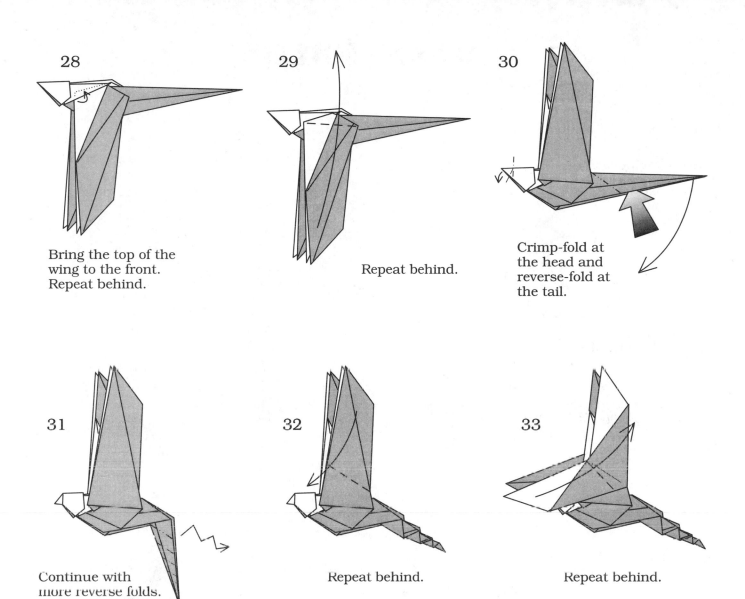

28

Bring the top of the wing to the front. Repeat behind.

29

Repeat behind.

30

Crimp-fold at the head and reverse-fold at the tail.

31

Continue with more reverse folds.

32

Repeat behind.

33

Repeat behind.

34

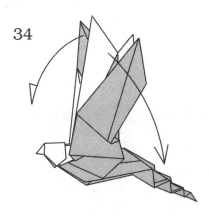

Spread the wings.

35

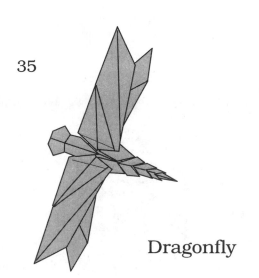

Dragonfly

BASIC FOLDS

Rabbit Ear.

To fold a rabbit ear, one corner is folded in half and laid down to a side.

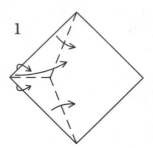

1

Fold a rabbit ear.

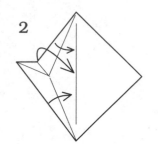

2

A three-dimensional intermediate step.

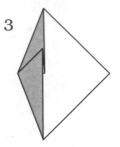

3

Double Rabbit Ear.

If you were to bend a straw you would be folding the double rabbit ear.

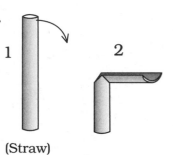

1   2

(Straw)

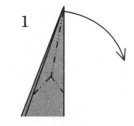

1

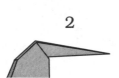

2

Make a double rabbit ear.

Squash Fold.

In a squash fold, some paper is opened and then made flat. The shaded arrow shows where to place your finger.

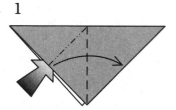

1

Squash-fold.

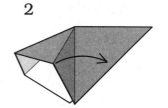

2

A three-dimensional intermediate step.

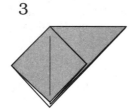

3

Petal Fold.

In a petal fold, one point is folded up while two opposite sides meet each other.

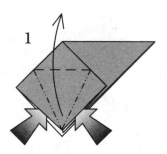

1

Petal-fold.

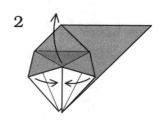

2

A three-dimensional intermediate step.

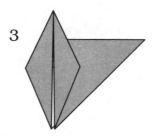

3

Inside Reverse Fold.

In an inside reverse fold, some paper is folded between layers. Here are two examples.

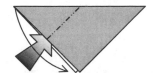

Reverse-fold.

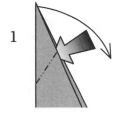

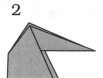

Reverse-fold.

Outside Reverse Fold.

Much of the paper must be unfolded to make an outside reverse fold.

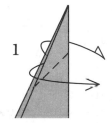

Outside-reverse-fold.

Crimp Fold.

A crimp fold is a combination of two reverse folds.

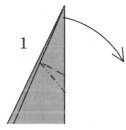

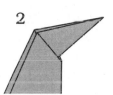

Crimp-fold.

Sink Fold.

In a sink fold, some of the paper without edges is folded inside. To do this fold, much of the model must be unfolded.

Sink.

Spread Squash Fold.

A cross between a squash fold and sink fold, some paper in the center is spread apart and then made flat.

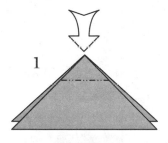

Spread-squash-fold.

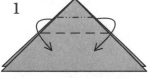

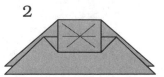

CREDITS

Creator	Models	Creator	Models
John Montroll	Tetrahedron Cube Diamond Evergreen Tree Swan (adaptation of a traditional model) Crane Vulture Goose Flamingo Pelican Alligator Tyrannosaurus Squirrel Aardvark Llama Bison	Gay Merrill Gross	George Washington Slept Here George Washington Framed Asian Dragon
		Stephen Hecht	"One-Way" Arrow Flower
Sy Chen	Boat Star of David Windmill House with Chimney	Mark Kennedy	Tulip
		Robert J. Lang	Peacock
Jim Cowling	Armadillo	Won Park	Eagle Butterfly Dragonfly
Stefan Delecat	Shirt with Tie	Matt Slayton	African Mask
Peter Farina	Sword Rabbit	Mike Thomas	Three Diamonds